ESSAYS FROM THE NEW ENG LAND ACADEM IC LIBRARI ANS' WRITING SEMINAR.

edited by
NORMAN D. STEVENS

The Scarecrow Press, Inc.
Metuchen, N.J., & London
1980

Library of Congress Cataloging in Publication Data

Main entry under title:

Essays from the New England Academic Librarians'
    Writing Seminar.

    The New England Academic Librarians' Writing Seminar
was a series of meetings held by professional librarians
in various places in New England over a two year period,
beginning in 1977, for the purpose of developing and
improving writing skills.
    Bibliography: p.
    1. Libraries, University and college--Addresses,
essays, lectures. 2. Library science--Addresses,
essays, lectures. I. Stevens, Norman D.
Z675.U5E78   027.7   80-21502
 ISBN 0-8108-1365-3

TABLE OF CONTENTS

iii

iv

FOREWORD

In the spring of 1976 the impressions of two experiences came together in my mind and led me to conceive of the idea of what came to be called the New England Academic Librarians' Writing Seminar. One experience had been negative; the other had been positive.

Earlier I had edited for The Scarecrow Press a volume entitled Essays for Ralph Shaw (1976). It was a series of papers written in honor of Shaw by my friends and classmates who had been Shaw's students in the doctoral program at the Rutgers University Graduate School of Library Service in the late 1950s and early 1960s. Despite the fact that we had all received sound training in research techniques and writing at Rutgers, and were presumably all highly motivated to contribute, it was an extremely difficult process to get the material gathered from a distance. Not everyone finally did contribute and those papers which I was ultimately able to gather needed more editing than the process allowed for. Except for the fact that the volume was finally published, it was not a rewarding experience.

On the other hand, I had then been participating on the Executive Committee of the New England Library Information Network (NELINET) for over five years. That experience, in which a group of librarians came together on a regular basis to act as a policy-making and advisory body for a large multi-state network, was a rewarding one. In that setting I had observed remarkable professional growth on the part of a number of people and an opportunity for librarians to work together in a productive way. Somehow, it seemed to me that if I could manage to bring together a group of librarians, in the kind of setting that NELINET allowed, we could then work together to develop and improve writing skills in a fashion that would alleviate some of the concerns I had had in attempting to edit the Shaw volume. Thus the concept of the New England Academic Librarians' Writing

Seminar, which is described in more detail in the Introduction and Appendix below, was formed.

I then wrote a letter to the Council on Library Resources, inquiring as to their possible interest in financially supporting such a program. Their initial response was favorable and subsequent correspondence with, and a visit to, the Council clarified a number of matters. That led to my writing a more detailed proposal which resulted in funding by the Council in the summer of 1976. In particular Dr. Stephen McCarthy, who was assigned responsibility by the Council for handling my proposal, was most helpful and contributed a number of useful ideas which helped strengthen the concept and the proposal.

In the fall of 1976 I solicited applications, reviewed those applications, selected the participants, and made arrangements for us to begin work. We did so early in 1977. As in any undertaking, things did not always move along as smoothly and as rapidly as might have been anticipated or desirable. In particular my heavy involvement in 1978 with the move to a major new library building at the University of Connecticut delayed completion of the work of the Seminar by a little more than six months. Nevertheless, as the bibliography of the Seminar writings below indicates, we did fairly rapidly produce articles for publication, and have produced a reasonable number of published pieces.

This volume represents the major and, in one sense, the final effort of the Seminar. It consists of the shorter essays we wrote for The Journal of Academic Librarianship and a series of longer essays prepared specifically for this book. In another sense this volume will, I hope, mark the beginning of the work of the Seminar. In the long run the Seminar will be a success if it marks the beginning, as I think it does, of long and productive careers in contributing to the literature of librarianship on the part of some, if not all, of the participants.

Norman D. Stevens

INTRODUCTION

The New England Academic Librarians' Writing Seminar

The following description of the New England Academic Librarians' Writing Seminar and the motivation behind it, the way it was organized, and the way it worked is based on the original proposal to the Council on Library Resources and the interim and final reports to the Council. For the sake of completeness that proposal and those reports are included as an appendix to this volume.

Background

The foreword has described the circumstances that led to the formation of the New England Academic Librarians' Writing Seminar. In large measure its formation was based on the assumption that there is a real need for an improvement in the quality of professional writing in the field of librarianship. It was also based on the assumption that there is a real need to develop contributions to the professional literature from a wider range of librarians. Certainly it is true that more and more librarians, especially academic librarians, find that their professional advancement is tied to publication. More importantly, however, it is increasingly clear that in order for professional librarians to maintain the kind of professional growth over a long career that is essential if they are to remain effective librarians, some kind of scholarly activity is highly desirable. The discipline that comes from writing is perhaps one of the most effective avenues for such activity.

The conditions that presently exist do not contribute to the development of writing skills among librarians. The basic program of graduate library education is perhaps the only point at which any emphasis is placed on the develop-

1

ment of writing skills.   That emphasis is obviously somewhat limited, in part because it assumes that people have already acquired such skills by the time they enter a graduate
program.   It is also not in a context in which writing is of
primary concern, and it tends to come too early in a person's
professional career.   Furthermore the writing of term papers,
or even of theses or dissertations, in a graduate library
school is not the same as writing for professional publication
and is not tested in the same critical way.   The present editorial practices of journal editors and publishers also do not
tend to contribute to an improvement of the situation.   In almost all cases proposed contributions tend to be accepted or
rejected on the basis of existing content and presentation.
Authors of items that are rejected are given little or no advice as to how the quality of their work could be improved.
Finally, the individual work environment and the normal professional contacts that a librarian has do not generally allow
for the development and improvement of writing skills.   Work
situations place most librarians in a directed setting where
the emphasis is on the content of the work and not on the
presentation of ideas.   At best a librarian may occasionally
be required to prepare a written report on some aspect of his/
her work.   In any case most librarians find themselves in
work situations which allow for only limited contact with other professional librarians, many of whom have either no interest in, or no particular ability for writing.   Professional
associations and activities are, for the most part, too large
and impersonal to allow for the development of adequate direct personal interrelationships which might have a real impact on the individual's professional growth and development
in this as in other areas.

     The result is that much of the professional growth
and development of professional librarians that involves writing skills takes place in an individual, unstructured framework, with relatively little opportunity for the individual to
discuss, test, and review his/her ideas, and the way in which
they are presented, before putting them into final form for
possible publication.   Learning to write for publication remains very much a chore that requires a high degree of
motivation and self-discipline, the ability to work independently, and an unusual level of interest in writing for publication.

     The New England Academic Librarians' Writing Sem-
inar was designed to help alleviate some of those problems
by seeking to establish a means whereby a group of ten to
twelve professional librarians in a reasonably compact geo-

graphic area could work together in a setting focussed specifically on the development and improvement of writing skills
through group interaction under the direction of a professional
librarian with demonstrated writing skills and abilities.   It
sought to provide an alternative means for the continuing education of the participants in a structured, yet relatively informal, setting that would provide a means for each participant to learn by criticizing the ideas and the writing of the
other participants and by having his/her ideas and writing
similarly criticized.

Initial Organization

        The primary function of the Seminar, as described in
the initial proposal, was thus to provide a setting in which
the written work of the individual participants could be reviewed and criticized by the other participants on a continuing basis.   It was felt that through such interaction and critical review the writing skills and abilities of the individuals
could be developed and improved.   It was also felt that, as
a result of such a process, the immediate end-product of
articles designed for publication could be improved significantly in quality.

        The initial proposal described how the Seminar might
function and, in large part, the measures described have
been followed.   Some of the working details were changed,
or evolved, as the Seminar operated and those details are
described further in the reports in the Appendix.   The basic
concept was simply that the group would meet on a regular
basis, normally one day a month, to review and criticize
the writing of each of the members.

        To support the focus on writing for publication, ar-
rangements were made with The Journal of Academic Librarianship to publish a series of brief essays under the
general heading "On Our Minds..." and with The Scarecrow
Press to publish this volume.

        As was indicated, support was sought, and was re-
ceived, from the Council on Library Resources to fund the
Seminar for a two-year period.   That support was designed
to pay for the travel expenses of the participants, to provide
for some part-time clerical support to assist in the handling
of the paperwork involved in administering the Seminar and,
especially, to provide for some typing assistance in the
preparation of manuscripts for publication.

Selection of Participants

        In the initial proposal the steps to be undertaken in
publicizing the Seminar and in selecting the participants were
described in some detail and those steps were essentially the
ones which were followed.

        Upon formal notification of the receipt of a grant from
the Council on Library Resources, immediate steps were taken
to publicize the grant in order to attract as large a number
of qualified applicants as possible. Both a news release and
a flyer describing the program were prepared and distributed.
The response was good and information about the Seminar appeared in a number of places.

        Despite those efforts the total number of applications
received was less than had been anticipated. Only 24 fully
completed applications, including three from outside New England, were received. On the basis of conversations with a
number of potential applicants, it appears that the requirements of the Seminar in terms of its time demands were high
enough to discourage many people. Perhaps a larger number
of applications would have been received if the program had
been of a shorter duration and involved less writing, or if it
had provided for financial support that would have allowed for
some released time from their normal duties for participants.

        Despite the limited number of applications, the quality
of those received was generally high. In the initial proposal
it had been indicated that one of the applicants with a good
previous writing background would be selected to serve as
Co-director of the Seminar. As it turned out none of the
applicants had had much previous writing experience and that
idea was dropped. Instead, after a careful initial review of
the applications, three of the candidates were selected for
participation and were asked to assist in the selection of the
remaining participants.

        By late 1976 all of the initial steps to organize the
Seminar had been completed and work began with a two-day
meeting held in early 1977.

Operation of the Seminar

        After that initial meeting the Seminar met on a regular
basis at locations throughout New England. While various

organizational and procedural topics were discussed at each of those meetings, the bulk of each meeting was devoted to a discussion of the ideas and the written expression of those ideas in papers prepared by the members. Normally, pieces were distributed prior to the meeting so that each participant had time to review and criticize material before coming to the meeting. The discussions were full and frank, and the group soon developed a good set of internal working relationships in which each member took an equal role. Emphasis tended to be placed on the ideas being presented and on how well they were stated rather than on matters of construction and grammar, although even those aspects of the writing came in for their share of criticism. The participants were encouraged to write as few or as many drafts as they felt necessary, and generally the decision that a piece was finished was a combination of individual decision and group consensus.

Only limited attention was formally paid to the question of publishing in the field of librarianship. A list of readings was prepared, the items were read, and there was a brief discussion about those items at an early meeting. In addition, as a result of that discussion and a general presentation by the Director about writing for publication, an article on the subject, which was reviewed and criticized in the Seminar, was written and has been published in Collection Management. Finally, John Berry, editor of Library Journal, and Richard Dougherty, editor of The Journal of Academic Librarianship, participated in meetings of the Seminar and shared with us many helpful ideas and suggestions from their perspective.

Accomplishments

The basic accomplishments of the New England Academic Librarians' Writing Seminar are the publications, including this volume, that we have produced. A complete listing of the publications resulting directly from the work of the Seminar is presented in the bibliography at the end of this volume.

Did we accomplish what we set out to do? Only time will tell. Obviously we feel that we have produced a number of written pieces of quality and it is certainly clear, from our experiences and observations, that the quality of those writings was substantially improved by being subjected to the process of review and criticism which we used. We hope that what we have had to say has been of value to others in the profession.

We did work together effectively as a group and developed a strong sense of friendship which resulted not only in the useful exchange of ideas but even in a practical short-term exchange of personnel between two of the libraries involved. We hope that the ties we have formed will endure and that we may continue to aid and assist one another in the exchange of ideas and the further improvement of our writing abilities. Finally, we each hope that the experience we have gained through this program will have enabled us to be more confident about our ability to express ourselves in writing, and that we will continue, over a period of time, to write for professional publication. If we do indeed do that, we will have accomplished what we set out to do.

New England Academic
Librarians' Writing Seminar

ON OUR MINDS...

INTRODUCTION

The following statements, which appeared in The Journal of Academic Librarianship at the start of the series of short essays, "On Our Minds...," by the members of the Seminar, summarize the purpose and intent of that series. The writing of relatively short pieces designed for publication as the initial work of the Seminar was felt, and proved to be, an excellent way of beginning the program. While it is difficult to express thoughts concisely, it is considerably easier to begin with attempting to write a short essay for publication than it is to attempt to write a longer piece which takes considerably more organizational skill.

On Our Minds--Writer's Seminar

"On Our Minds" is a series of brief commentaries on a range of academic library concerns, both old and new, developed by members of the New England Academic Librarians' Writing Seminar. We are a small group of academic librarians brought together, under a grant from the Council on Library Resources, by the fact that we work in New England and share a common concern about the need to improve our ability to express our thoughts to others in writing.

We will be meeting regularly over a two-year period to review and criticize each other's ideas and the written expression of those ideas. Although we will be working together, uniformity of opinion or presentation is not our goal. We simply hope to help each other prepare for publication contributions which are of high quality both substantively and stylistically.

This series will be one concrete result of the Seminar. Another will be a collection of longer essays which is to be published by The Scarecrow Press sometime in 1979. In addition the Seminar participants will pursue a number of individual writing activities.

Writing achieves its purpose only when it expresses ideas clearly and concisely and when it stimulates the thinking of others. Let us know how well we are succeeding. Let us know what is on your mind.

Norman D. Stevens

Editor's Note

When Norman Stevens invited JAL to participate in his writing seminar, we were delighted to accept. More than a decade of reading poorly-organized, awkwardly written manuscripts convinced me that Stevens' proposal was long overdue. Of course, one seminar won't cure the writing malaria that afflicts our profession, but it might raise the consciousness toward the problem. The model proposed could be applied by library schools, individual libraries, or local library clubs.

The writing seminar, in my opinion, provides an enviable opportunity for a group of promising librarians to improve their communication skills. JAL is pleased to serve as a forum for their work. The papers will be published unedited, as they were submitted. We think our readers will find them both readable and informative.

Richard M. Dougherty

HOW TO HIRE A LIBRARY DIRECTOR:
THE EREWHON EXPERIENCE

by Wes Daniels

The librarians at Erewhon State University were over-joyed when they learned that three of them had been named to the Search Committee for a Director of the University Library. The last time a Director had been hired, ten years earlier, the librarians hadn't even been consulted, much less given a voice in recommending a candidate to the President.

At the Search Committee's first meeting, the librarians took their seats around the table with the three faculty members, two administrators, two undergraduates and one graduate student who were to be their Committee colleagues. The group decided to advertise the position nationally and to interview the three most promising applicants.

The three finalists were flown to Erewhon on three successive days. They were scrutinized by the Committee at morning and afternoon sessions of an hour each, sandwiched around a two-hour lunch with the University President and the Vice-President for Academic Affairs. A tour of the campus, afternoon tea with the professional library staff, and a walk through the Technical Services Department and the stacks rounded out the day's activities.

After taking the weekend to think the situation over, the Committee reconvened the following Monday and voted to forward to the President the résumés of the three candidates, ranked in order to preference.

A month later, the President announced the appointment as Director of the University Library the administrator who had been the Committee's second choice. Rumor had it that their preferred candidate had been unable to negotiate a satisfactory salary.

Before long, serious problems with the new Director developed. The clerical workers union filed several grievances against him. A number of professional staff members announced their departure from Erewhon for other jobs (including two of the librarians who had served on the Search Committee). Even the President's secretary was having a hard time scheduling a meeting with the Director, who always seemed to be away on a trip somewhere.

For his part, the Director had rapidly become disenchanted. Money for his budget was a lot less forthcoming than he had been led to believe. He was being forced to place people with political connections in library positions. Several ill-advised decisions of his predecessor had to be revoked, and his allotment of work-study students had been cut in half.

In the middle of the second semester, the Director announced to a library staff meeting that he was leaving at the end of his first academic year.

A group of interested librarians and support staff began meeting to come up with some ideas about how to avoid a repetition of the previous year's mistakes. The following memo was the result of their deliberations:

TO: President, Erewhon State University
FROM: Ad Hoc Library Committee
SUBJECT: Hiring a Library Director

We are concerned that the problems of the past year have resulted, in part, from flaws in the process used to hire the Library Director.

Most of the problems seem to have resulted from two basic facts: when the Director was hired, we knew too little about him and he knew too little about us. In an attempt to avoid repeating the same mistakes, we offer the following suggestions:

1. Library support staff should be represented on the Search Committee. Support staff can offer a valuable and unique perspective. They are often the people who have been around the longest and are therefore most familiar with the history of the library and the evolution of its policies and procedures. They are also the ones who actually make the machinery run--either smoothly or otherwise. For the li-

brary to accomplish its purpose, harmonious relations between the Director and staff are essential.

    2. Librarians and support staff should comprise a
majority of the Search Committee. Simply stated, faculty,
students, and administrators cannot hope to be as knowledge-
able about the operations of the library--either actual or po-
tential--as those who operate it. Further, those whose lives
are to be the most directly affected by the choice of a Director should have a significant voice in that selection.

    3. The role of the Search Committee should be well
defined. Among the functions specifically delegated to the
Committee should be: preparation of the job description and
requirements; responsibility for taking affirmative steps to
locate qualified candidates if advertising alone fails to produce
an adequate pool; establishment of the criteria for choosing
those applicants who are to be interviewed, and of the format
of the interviews; establishment of the criteria for evaluating
those interviewed; and participation in the negotiations with
the librarian to whom the position is offered.

    4. The Search Committee should undergo training be-
fore beginning its work. Without proper preparation, the
Committee might very well function in an overly haphazard
or subjective manner, and fail to elicit the data necessary to
make informed decisions. Faculty from the School of Management, for example, could educate the Committee members in
effective methods of defining criteria, establishing procedures,
and conducting interviews.

    5. As many candidates as possible should be inter-
viewed. There is an art to writing an impressive-sounding
résumé; how much can you really tell from a piece of paper?
It is a false economy to "save" money by cutting down on the
number of people whose travel expenses have to be paid by
the University. The person chosen will be responsible for
the expenditure of millions of dollars, and will have a significant impact on the development of a major sector of the
University. A few hundred dollars is a wise investment if it
means finding the best available candidate.

    6. Applicants should be given a chance to investigate
our library and our University. A whirlwind, one-day stay
filled with planned activities serves this function poorly.
There are a number of ways in which this could be improved.
The means chosen would have to depend on the individual's

situation.   Some universities, when considering employing
faculty members permanently in key positions will offer a
prospective choice a visiting professorship for a semester or
for a full academic year.   Mutual evaluation of the faculty
member and the institution can then take place over a meaningful period of time.   This, of course, will not always be
feasible in the hiring of a library Director.   At the very
least, however, each finalist could be offered the chance to
"reside" at the University for a week or two, and thus be
able to more systematically and realistically find out what
type of situation he would encounter in coming to work here.
This time might also be used to ask the candidate to study
and report on a specific problem, perhaps on a consultant
basis.

        7.   Candidates' current places of employment should
be investigated.   Although an interview can tell you more than
a résumé, not much in-depth knowledge of a person's capabilities can be gained from a couple of hours of questions.
What the applicant says is important; what he has actually
done is even more critical.   An individual or team could be
sent to the place where each of the finalists now works to
talk to the candidate in his setting and to get a first-hand
look at the library at which he has most recently practiced
his librarianship.   Staff members at these libraries should
be consulted.   (Strict guidelines, however, must be followed.
The initial job advertisements should state explicitly that in-
terviewees' places of employment may be visited, and the
Committee must be careful to establish in advance the questions to be asked to prevent even the inadvertent collection
of inappropriate information.)

        These proposals are meant to generate discussion to-
ward the formulation of a more productive search policy.
Please let us know what you think of them.

THE ACADEMIC LIBRARY IN A
"SCHOOLED" SOCIETY

by Susan L. Lindgren

In today's schooled society, [1] librarians and other educators view libraries as institutions which facilitate access to
education. This view makes the library a convivial institution, that is, one which exists to be used. "The rules which
govern it have mainly the purpose of avoiding abuses which
would frustrate their general accessibility" (DS, p. 79). In
the ideal sense, the library should be an institution which
allows individuals to function independently in a supportive
learning environment.

The extreme opposite of the convivial institution is the
manipulative institution. These institutions "tend to develop
effects contrary to their aims"; membership is obtained by
coercion, and the participation in and consumption of services
is involuntary (DS, pp. 78-9). The school, from the elementary grades to the university, is a manipulative institution.

The schooled society has set a goal for the individual:
the attainment of education status through proper institutional
channels which require attendance, tests, grades, certificates,
and degrees. It maintains these requirements despite incon-
clusive evidence of their relationship to the amount of learning that occurs within educational institutions, and in light of
much empirical data attesting to their unreliability.

How can the library be a convivial resource when it
is attached to an educational system based on obligations and
compulsions? How is the library perceived by education con-
sumers accustomed to a schooled society where it is generally accepted that learning is the result of teaching, where self-
instruction is neither highly regarded nor rewarded, and
where promotion is based on securing credentials instead of
knowledge? To students locked into the requirements of an
educational institution the library can be as manipulative and
coercive as its supporting system.

Professional teachers laugh at the idea that people
would learn more from random access to learning
resources than they can be taught. In fact, they
frequently cite as proof for their skepticism the
declining use of libraries. They overlook the fact
that libraries are little used because they have
been organized as formidable teaching devices.
Libraries are not used because people have been
trained to demand that they be taught (TC, p. 70).

The user's perception of the academic library is dependent on several factors, including: predisposition to learning; degree of interest; motivation; and position in the academic hierarchy. That perception is based, primarily, on
conditions and factors external to the library itself. The organization of the library, its rules and regulations, the nature
of the collection, and the responsiveness of the staff may work
to reinforce or alter those perceptions. Most often, the image is reinforced.

Those who perceive the library as a convivial institution have a fairly high rating in all, or most, of the above
categories: they see the library as one of many possible resources to increase their knowledge; they are propelled by a
genuine interest in learning a fact or understanding a subject;
most likely, they are free of the pressures of a grade-oriented
approach to acquiring knowledge. It is evident that this group
comprises a minority of the campus community: i. e. , the
faculty, with some exceptions, and a handful of other, persistent learners. Within this select group, faculty members
have a distinct advantage; their academic rank removes most
of the institutional barriers that thwart the average patron,
the undergraduate. Without the obstacles and the frustrations,
without the apathy stemming from compulsory learning, the
image of the library as a convivial institution can exist.
Though the individuals within this group function in the schooled
society, their interests, motivations, and status alleviate the
pressures of that society.

Undergraduates, comprising the majority of the campus
population, are more likely to perceive and use the library as
a manipulative institution than as a convivial one. The library
is a place to study and complete assignments. Most students
have been taught, through years of primary and secondary
schooling, to use their minds as information receptacles to
hold prepackaged units of knowledge. They increase their
knowledge primarily through the faculty member as an information resource as well as through course readings which

he/she assigns. They memorize information under pressures
produced by constraints of time and grades.   They may proceed through an assignment, course, or entire degree program enticed by credits and diplomas, stockpiling credentials
for the ultimate reward, the job. Throughout the degree program the library is used as an adjunct to courses. From
the average undergraduate's point of view, the library is a
learning resource only insofar as it provides answers to questions someone else has asked. What can the library provide
that will fulfill the requirements of the course? Fulfilling
these requirements carries the promise of reward; satisfying
one's curiosity does not.

        Institutional barriers based on the undergraduate's
academic status, or lack of it, reinforce the manipulative
view of the library. With all of this conditioning it is understandable that so few students use the library to encourage
free thinking and learning. Learning is work; and time not
spent on assignments will not be spent in the library.

        How do the operations in a library reinforce such ex-
treme images? Policies and practices in acquisitions, reference, interlibrary loan, and circulation are responsible.
The traditions are based on the premise that the faculty member, as a serious learner, is worthy of privileges and benefits. The undergraduate, whose devotion to learning is sus-
pect, must be kept in line by stricter rules. The student,
caught in the acts of writing and "researching" minutes before
an assignment is due, is often seen in an unflattering light.

        The library collection is developed to support the cur-
riculum by order of acquisitions policies. Careful selection
is done to obtain a collection which will serve as an adjunct
to the courses offered. Books are not routinely acquired for
subjects that are not taught. While sound in budgetary principle, this policy discourages self-instruction outside of a
set curriculum. A student wishing to learn a foreign language,
for example, may not find a self-teaching manual or grammar
in the library if that language is not offered at the institution.
A faculty member, on the other hand, helps develop the collection in his/her own fields of interest. Collection support
is not assured for the student to the same degree that it is
for the faculty member.

        Some types of reference service follow the same con-
vivial versus manipulative pattern. When reference librarians
provide bibliographic instruction to classes at the request of

an instructor, the sessions are usually geared to a specific course or assignment. Attendance is urged if not compulsory. Boredom and disinterest are evident to the librarian who is quick to note inattentiveness and lack of response. If the librarian uses highly relevant examples in the card catalog, periodical indexes, statistical compilations, or other sources attention is momentarily increased; the student is attuned to answers since answers lead to better grades.

A student seeking material for a term paper may be advised to change topics when the library collection is found lacking. The student's interest in the subject is not a factor worthy of extensive consideration. It is unlikely that a similar suggestion would be made to a faculty member engaged in research when the library collection lacks needed materials. Instead elaborate steps may be undertaken to assist him/her in identifying appropriate material through specialized literature searches. Time, knowledge, and ability to search the literature are obstacles to the student; for the privileged faculty member or administrator, time, knowledge, and ability are problems left to the librarian.

Even if the student persists in tracking down material on a subject of interest that is not owned by the library it does little good. The manipulative versus the convivial nature of the library is most evident in interlibrary loan codes and practices. The 1968 National Interlibrary Loan Code of the American Library Association states: "requests for individuals with academic affiliations should be limited to those materials needed for faculty and staff research, and the thesis and dissertation research of graduate students." Requests from faculty, however, are rarely scrutinized or challenged on the basis of intended use of the item. Interlibrary loan requests from undergraduates are discouraged; the student's right to learn is abridged. Requests for material relating to the student's personal interests, rather than course work, are rarely accepted. While exceptions may be made for undergraduate requests that are related to course "research," those exceptions most often require the signature of the faculty member teaching the course, indicating approval of the material and/or subject to be studied. State or regional interlibrary loan codes may be more responsive to undergraduate needs, though they, too, concentrate on course related material. Academic interlibrary loan policies sanction undergraduate learning only when that learning is accompanied by tuition payments for courses.

Circulation rules and regulations reinforce the convivial library image for faculty.   Services such as extended or unlimited loan periods, private study carrels or lounges, and access to closed stack areas decrease the privileged users' frustrations.   For other patrons lack of status offers stiff overdue fines, crowded and/or noisy seating areas, and delays caused by closed stack collections.   Special libraries or collections may be available only to those individuals with the proper credentials or identification.   A juvenile book collection, for example, may be accessible only to students in a children's literature course; a special library may be restricted to students enrolled in the proper school or college of the university.

The extreme images of the academic library as a convivial or manipulative institution, held by faculty and undergraduates, respectively, will not account for the perceptions of every individual.   As circumstances and individuals change, so do perceptions.   There are faculty members who feel thwarted and abused by library operations just as there are students who thrive in the library environment.   Restrictions are placed on uncooperative faculty and exceptions are made for persistent, dedicated students.   But as long as the academic library reinforces the attitudes toward learning created by a schooled society, its basic image will be predictable.

Note

1. See Ivan Illich's Deschooling Society (N. Y.:   Harper, 1970) and Tools for Conviviality (N. Y.:   Harper, 1973).   The concept of manipulative versus convivial institutions and the quotations in this essay are from his works.

COLLECTION DEVELOPMENT: THE RIGHT
AND RESPONSIBILITY OF LIBRARIANS

by Bonnie Naifeh Hill

If we are ever to establish ourselves as a profession
rather than just highly-trained functionaries; if we are ever
to become the doctors instead of the nurses; the scientists
instead of the lab technicians; we must stand up for our ability to perform decision-making work rather than just the implementation of those decisions. The first step is a belief
in our ability to make those decisions, especially when it
comes to the primary reason for our professional existence--
the collection itself.

Most writings are concerned primarily with determining value by use, and various ways are suggested to do this.
None advocates the use of a title-by-title approach to selection and retention of materials which proceeds in a logical
manner based on the philosophical position that only librarians
have the expertise to make final decisions on the composition
of a collection in any given library. The segments of the
library world--authors, educators, practitioners, and re-
searchers--seem content to leave such an approach in limbo
by declaring that local conditions in any institution are so
unique that anything more than vast, sweeping generalizations
about collection development could not apply to more than, at
most, a handful of libraries, and so they are best not dealt
with at all. There often follows, fast on the heels of such
an assertion, the assurance that such knowledge can and will
be learned on the job. While immediately comforting, this
usually is not true, and we, individually and collectively, are
left with an empty arsenal to defend our collection-building
attempts and diminishing budgets. Librarians are judged by
others and, far too often, by themselves to be lacking in the
skills, knowledge, and ability to shoulder these responsibilities.
The most widespread approach to collection development seems
to be to leave it in the hands of the faculty with the librarian
filling in the gaps as funds allow.

20   ON OUR MINDS...

        At the same time, there is increasing professional
pressure for librarians to take hold of their library's development in such a manner as to predict it, plan it, and, to
some degree, control it. In the area of collection development, this pressure manifests itself, in one way, in the ever-
growing emphasis on book-selection policies. The growing
trend and the age old practice seem to be mutually exclusive;
for why should one group make decisions for another? Further, how do librarians who are attempting to codify and articulate collection development translate this attempt into
forceful and telling budgetary requests which support orderly
and valid growth when they lack the final authority to implement such growth? Finally, how do librarians, working under
the status quo, keep up with the changing goals, priorities
and emphases of the university in order to maintain the relevance and usefulness of these policies if they are merely in
a position of reaction rather than of decision? Even more,
why should they bother?

        It is essential to evaluate the development of a collec-
tion as it proceeds as well as at periodic intervals. It is
also necessary to determine that development so that the best
possible end result is obtained. It should not, in other words,
just grow like Topsy. Unfortunately, this has happened all
too often--due, largely, to faculty control over what is purchased. It is time for everyone to question this practice.

        Why are faculty deemed capable of collection develop-
ment? The typical faculty member teaches perhaps a maximum of five courses and has a specialty in one or two areas
of a specific subject discipline. How do such credentials
prepare someone to speak knowledgeably on all areas of
learning as they relate to all information appearing in any
particular form? The fact is that no one has such credentials. Rather than coming up with some method of dealing
with the problem, librarians have allowed faculty to assume
this power, and then they complain when the faculty doesn't
do it or does it poorly. Consider that this responsibility
isn't even rightfully theirs; they are engaged primarily to
train persons in a specific subject discipline, not to build
and judge library collections.

        It is our responsibility, and I believe that with effort
we can evolve an intelligent way of dealing with it. We should
assume that the librarian is capable of collection development.
The library organization provides for the development of subject specialists with the further specialized knowledge of the

book trade, both foreign and domestic, to a much greater
degree than any other academic unit; for it can structure
some of its positions to be exclusively responsible for collection development.   No other unit of the university can le-
gitimately make this claim.

I do not maintain that every librarian selecting materials would, could, or should read everything that is purchased in its entirety.   But then, neither does the faculty
member who is selecting materials read everything.   Reasons
for purchase extend beyond the factual content of any item.
A scholar's opinion is also considered a valid area of academic study as is the refutation of that opinion by some other
scholar.   In certain areas, political science and religion being outstanding examples, the whole gamut of opinion is even
more important than the factual content.   The librarian is in
an even better position here than is the faculty member for
he or she has no vested interest in any one school of thought
and can, therefore, avoid to a greater degree unconscious
censorship.

Reasons for sensible, organized, centralized collection
development abound.   Reasons for augmenting the librarian's
role abound.   This is one way to begin to achieve both goals.

THE UNITED STATES NONDEPOSITORY LIBRARY:
A COMMENDATION

by Elisabeth S. Burns

The breadth and scope of U. S. government publications
makes them an essential part of the information service offered by any academic library. Many college and university
libraries have taken advantage of the opportunity to become
depositories. But not all academic libraries are eligible, for
geographical or other reasons, to join the depository system,
and some do not wish to join. These nondepositories miss
the benefits of the deposit system, but they also avoid the
responsibilities established by law. Yet there is no reason
why the nondepository should not have a satisfactory number
of federal documents to enrich its total collection, and it is
far more free to follow its own inclinations in the selection,
arrangement, and eventual disposal of this material.

The main difficulty is to get started. The first attempt
to select government publications may be a traumatic experience for the librarian trained in the acquisition of regular
trade books. In the small academic library, which does not
receive blanket shipments of books in any field, or from any
particular presses, and which relies heavily on reviews for
book buying, the purchase of documents will seem, at first,
a leap in the dark. Considering the amount of material published, the reviewing is negligible. The review system
doesn't even pretend to be current. A title reviewed in 1976
may originally have been produced in 1972. Since much of
the material is of immediate interest, this is too great a
time lag for a selection policy based on reviews. Nothing
like Choice or Library Journal exists for government publications. The Reference Quarterly (RQ) has a short column;
each issue of Government Publications Review and Documents
to the People (DTTP) reviews five or six titles. The acquisitions librarian soon discovers that government publications
differ from trade books in one important respect. Documents
do not compete with one another. The titles purchased should

be those which will support the curriculum, and will make
the total library collection more effective.   If the statistical
results of the 1970 Census of Population are needed, the library will buy, without further investigation, the U. S. Bureau
of the Census compilation of those statistics.

But reviews can serve other purposes.   Occasionally
in DTTP an entire series is analyzed (the Federal Statistics
Series of the U. S. Department of Commerce, for example),
giving an excellent picture of how the parts fit together as a
whole and providing valuable information about titles which
have not recently been reissued or updated.   The announce-
ment of forthcoming series and other new publications in
DTTP is also helpful.

The acquisitions process always requires careful consideration, particularly in documents.   Basic material may
be culled from annotated bibliographies like Government Reference Books: A Biennial Guide to U. S. Government Publications, compiled by Alan Edward Schorr (formerly by Sally
Wynkoop); or the Annotated List of Selected United States
Government Publications Available to Depository Libraries,
by Sylvia Mechanic.   Standing orders for annuals and other
serial publications may be placed with a jobber.   A deposit
account may be opened, and items not handled by the jobber
may be chosen from the Selected U. S. Government Publications and the Monthly Catalog.

Not everything that is ordered will arrive.   There is
no way an agency can calculate how many copies of a given
title should be printed to satisfy public demand.   At times
the supply is insufficient, and it is a case of first come,
first served.   Stocks may run out at the Government Documents Distribution Centers.   It is not uncommon to order five
months items and receive three.   The fourth may come six
later, the fifth, never.   If the out-of-stock title is a depository item, it will at least be held by a local depository.   If
it is not a depository item, it may be forever unattainable,
except on a short-term basis through interlibrary loan.

Bibliographic citations can be a problem for the nondepository librarian.   This is no reflection on those who have
worked so hard in recent years to establish bibliographic control of government publications.   It is rather an indictment
of people who write books and do not include all the necessary
components of a documents imprint in the bibliography.   The
addition of author and title indexes to the Monthly Catalog has

greatly increased its usefulness for finding items listed since
1974, but anything before that can still be difficult, especially
if the issuing agency is not given.   The librarian who is asked
to obtain federal documents cited in a 1972 publication, either
by purchasing the items from GPO, or requesting them through
interlibrary loan, may have a hard time.   The citations may
be by author and title, in which case an educated guess must
be made as to the original source of the publication, or simply by number, as, for example, NTIS Report #12.   Considering the sheer volume of NTIS Reports, this is not enlight-
ening.   One should ask the nearest depository for assistance.

        Most depository libraries use the Superintendent of
Documents classification, and set up a separate documents
collection, with its own full-time staff.   Most nondepositories
integrate government publications with the main book collection, and use whatever classification scheme is applicable.
There may be a number of reasons for this.   The nondepository library may feel that it does not purchase enough federal
documents to justify separate housing.   It may not wish to
employ the extra staff that would be needed to handle a special collection.   (The budget may be a factor here, too.
There may not be enough money for additional personnel.)
Most importantly, it may think that in a nondepository situation, documents would not be used as much if they were
housed in a separate area.

        There are definite advantages to integrated housing.
When government publications are shelved in the general
stacks, they are far more accessible to the patron.   Those
people who would normally shy away from the very mention
of the words "government documents" will begin to use them
as a matter of course.   The librarians themselves develop
greater familiarity with the information documents can supply,
and greater expertise in using them.   Access to the documents probably extends over a longer period of time.   They
are available whenever the library is open, rather than from
8:30 to 4:30, or for that one night in the week the documents
librarian may be on duty as part of the rotating evening staff.

        Being a nondepository, therefore, has definite com-
pensations.   There is no inspection.   The nondepository is
free to house federal documents as it wishes, use any classification scheme it finds suitable, and dispose of the documents as it wishes.   Often a larger percentage proportion of
the professional librarians is able to use this material effectively.   Finally, the nondepository library staff should experi-

ence the satisfaction of knowing that the college community as a whole is using documents regularly, in addition to books and periodical articles, and is generally becoming aware of the wealth of information available from the U.S. Government.

IN SEARCH OF A PANACEA

by Karen A. Littlefield

"Will you walk into my parlor?"
said the Spider to the Fly. *

A spider's web is a beautifully simple thing in its
complexity: an open, symmetrical, and strong structure
created for and fulfilling a purpose. A library is often seen
by its patrons as a web that entraps and keeps them from
their purpose. They also often see the librarian as the spider whose only purpose is to spin the sticky threads that
bind. Unfortunately, librarians frequently behave as if this
were true; and, in fact, many believe that it is true.

A public library may follow the Spider's example and
use "wily, flattering words, " or follow Charlotte A. Cavatica's
example and weave enchanting messages into the design of
the web to entice reluctant patrons, most of whom have a
choice to enter or not. An academic library may do the
same. However, the academic library has a ready-made
clientele which, although there are always exceptions, must
come into the web. Whether or not librarians emulate the
Spider's beguiling ways or Charlotte's exceptional skill at
spinning, they should at least have Charlottian patience, practicality, and wisdom in dealing with problems.

Yet at times it seems that librarians deliberately make
simple things complex. It is as if they were no longer ra-
tional human beings with an acquired expertise but spiders
who spin by instinct. In itself, this phenomenon would not be
particularly noteworthy. However, many librarians seem to
have lost the innate sense of pattern and the ability to stop
spinning when the web is complete. This may be changing.
Influences from the "outside world, " particularly from the
business world, have appeared inside the library. With all

*Mary Howitt, "The Spider and the Fly: An Apologue. "

their good as well as all their bad aspects, things such as
advertising, participatory management, and other techniques
have begun to change the image of the library and the librarian.

   Computerization is one of the latest tools from the
business world to become part of the library world. Computers are now considered so important to libraries and their
operation that instruction in computer systems is advocated
as a necessary part of library school education and, in some
cases, actually is part of it. For those librarians who have
not had the advantage of such courses in their curriculum,
there is an abundance of workshops, seminars, congresses,
and conferences to help them catch up. The complex machinery that is a computer is looked upon as something that will
make all things simple. There is hope, and even some evidence, that the computer will be a panacea for illnesses in-
fecting libraries.

>   "'Tis the prettiest little parlor
>   that ever you did spy;
>   The way into my parlor is up a
>   winding stair,
>   And I've many curious things to
>   show when you are there. "

   Librarians have begun to shed what has seemed to
some their ugly image as spider and have turned the web-
spinning duties over to computers or are programming computers toward this end. Acquisitions, cataloging, circulation,
and reference are the most obvious examples of areas in
which computers now have a large role. There are many
other library functions that could be handled by computer systems: some of these are being studied; some are about to
be implemented. Smaller libraries without access to local
computer systems may not have had all the advantages the
larger libraries have had unless they belong to a cooperative
network group. But small libraries have benefited from the
national systems which are available, particularly in cataloging, acquisitions, and interlibrary loan.

   While the patron may still have little comprehension
of the mysterious processes that occur to make "his" book
ready to be signed out and cares less what the processes
are (as long as they work), he seems impressed. Still,
somewhat in awe of machine systems that can tell him which
books are ready for use, which books are in use, and can
also save him time in the dull routine of searching biblio-

graphic tools, patrons are convinced that libraries and librarians do, and should, exist in the twentieth century. If the patrons are happy, the librarians are at least happier.

In a time when libraries are being pressured by the rapid proliferation of knowledge, by lack of space, time, and money, and by increased demands for service, it is easy to understand why librarians have turned to computers. Yet it should be noted that while the essence of spiders and spiders' webs is considered by practitioners of folk-medicine to be a cure for some afflictions (particularly infantile ones), they are also an important ingredient in the practice of witchcraft.

> "Oh no, no," said the little Fly,
>   "to ask me is in vain,
> For who goes up your winding stair
>   can ne'er come down again."

Computers may not take over the world. In spite of this promise by computer advocates, it is frightening to look through periodicals devoted exclusively to literature about computers and realize just how far the computer invasion has progressed. In addition to sorting, storing, printing, and projecting varieties of economic sociological, medical, and historical data, and in addition to widespread use in industry and commerce, already computers are also musicians, artists, and poets. They create beauty; they are beautiful! Computers are recreational (providing both traditional and unique games); they are a craft (build one's own); maybe they will be a hobby (collect them). One individual was even conducting a survey to ascertain the humanistic qualities of computers.

Despite their ominous presence, computers eventually may not take over libraries. However, to the extent that they are already in libraries, they may be making inadequate situations worse. Like the black widow spider, the computer is spinning a truly tangled web, and even the librarians are becoming caught in it.

What happens when computer systems fail to perform to promised and expected standards or fail to perform altogether? If, for example, an existing acquisition program cannot be made to work when it is switched to a larger computer, the ordering function is all but paralyzed. Books cannot be ordered; those received cannot be acknowledged; accounts cannot be paid; the status of funds is unknown. The addition of computer services has reduced the size of the staff, and it is too cumbersome to go back to manual ordering. The cataloging department is affected, for it cleaned up its backlog of books during the acquisitions department's previous computer failures. Even if cataloging had books, efficiency would not be noticeable, for the cataloging computer system has its own bugs: extended downtimes, progressive slowdown in response time, elimination of some search modes, and lists that must be consulted to avoid searching for something with too many entries. In addition, while the data base is rapidly increasing, the quality of records is decreasing; the amount of time spent on one book increases as it passes from nonprofessional to paraprofessional to professional. Here, too, the human staff has been cut because of the computer.

Cost to the patron or institution places limitations on the accessibility of data bases available to the reference department. The additional time spent by the librarian training the patron in the search strategy and the time spent acting as mediator between the patron and the computer is time which could be spent guiding several other patrons to the bibliographic tools.

There may be some justification for replacing people with machines, but there is something of a paradox in it. Money saved on salaries is invested in computer services, but computer systems and the accompanying machinery are rapidly outmoded, as well as increasingly more expensive each time they must be replaced. Salaries for human workers may increase from year to year, but people can be retrained. While one machine may be able to do the work of several people, a few people are responsible for pushing the same amount of work through the system. And the computer is not doing its fair share.

There is also a social issue involved. Human labor, which is always available, can be trained to meet the institution's needs; the institution must be trained to need only that which the computer can provide. In addition to the increasingly wide availability of nonprofessional, as well as professional, labor, library schools are still granting degrees in great numbers in the face of a decreasing job market. And while computers are not the only reason for the present job situation, they are a contributing factor.

Advocates of computer technology in libraries may

feel that acceptance of computers has been too slow.   Con-
vincing them that it has not been slow enough is a problem.
In the case of computers being or becoming a panacea for
library problems, the illnesses may have fewer unpleasant
consequences than the cure.   As the black widow destroys
her mate, the computer may be the death of the librarian,
unless he finds an antidote.

> Unto an evil counsellor, close
>   heart, and ear, and eye,
> And take a lesson from this tale,
>   of the Spider and the Fly.

FACULTY LIBRARY PRIVILEGES

by Dorothy Kijanka

Dealing with the faculty in an academic library is sometimes looked upon by librarians as an adversary relationship. Librarians think that faculty members expect preferential treatment which the library is not prepared to give. Some faculty members do indeed believe that their status enables them to receive services that are not given to other members of the academic community. Greater privileges were granted to faculty in the past on the assumption that their status gave rise to greater need, but this tradition is slowly changing. Even many faculty members now recognize that the needs of others for library services may be as valid as their own.

Traditionally, faculty have enjoyed privileges ranging from control of book selection and unrestricted borrowing to separate restrooms and telephones. The faculty find a rationale for all of these needs based on the value of their time, labor, and contribution to their school, profession, and society. Faculty members who are preparing books or articles for publication may need to keep library materials longer than students who are writing term papers. Faculty feel they must take part in the book selection process to ensure that library holdings support their courses and research. They may need a quiet place to study and write or free access to materials and a place to store them. Even access to private restrooms and telephones can be rationalized by faculty on the grounds that special consideration should be given them because their time is valuable.

Similar arguments, however, can be made on behalf of other members of the university community. The completion of a term paper or thesis may be as important to the future of a student as the publication of an article or book is to the career of a faculty member. Although the pressures of publication on administrators are not as great, they often need to prepare reports, speeches, and articles which may require the use of library services and materials. The needs for research and writing are similar in substance if different in degree, and the time expended and contributions made by each segment of the community are valuable. The solution to the problem lies not in automatically denying all special privileges to faculty but in extending some of these same privileges to others on the basis of need and in withdrawing special privileges when no clear need exists or when those privileges impinge on the legitimate needs of other users.

One of the greatest distinctions still made by academic libraries between faculty and students is the amount of time each may borrow material. It may range from two weeks for students to no time-limit for faculty. This discrimination is perpetuated by the tradition of granting special privileges to faculty and reinforced by the practical problems of getting the books back into the library. Students ultimately can be forced to return and pay for materials by the withholding of grades, transcripts, and diplomas. It is more difficult to exert control over faculty, and not setting a due date for faculty loans is an easy solution to the problem. If, however, the library wishes to have the books available to all users, it will have to make loan periods the same for everyone and attempt to get the books back from everyone. Methods that may be adopted are imposition of fines and charges, refusal of further borrowing privileges, and the replacement of unreturned materials from departmental book funds. Not all of these methods are successful with faculty. The fine system will not work unless there is some way to ensure payment, and that is often impossible. The refusal of borrowing privileges until library obligations are met is an extremely difficult system to maintain. Replacing unreturned materials from departmental book funds will make the materials available to all users even though this policy may not influence faculty members to return other items in the future.

Another privilege usually reserved for faculty but not always intelligently used is control of book selection. The disadvantages of faculty selection, especially combined with tight departmental allocations, are well known. Yet a library may rely almost entirely for book selection on faculty requests, no matter how esoteric, while student requests are usually ignored as being out of scope. Requests for material should be evaluated on their own merits and not on the basis of the status of the persons making requests.

A quiet place for study and research is everyone's goal, especially since libraries are no longer places where silence is strictly maintained.   Private studies where research and writing may be done in comparative quiet and where materials may be stored should be available to all serious researchers, whether on a daily, weekly, or a semester basis.   They should be continued only where reasonable use is demonstrated.   Easy access to materials should similarly be provided on the basis of need.   Closed stacks should not be open only to faculty or doctoral students but to other graduate students and undergraduates doing serious research.   These are privileges that should be shared equally by all who can demonstrate a legitimate need.

Faculty should not have their questions answered before everyone else's at the reference desk, nor should they have their books checked out at the head of the line at the circulation desk.   These are truly unwarranted privileges, and because no special need exists they should be withdrawn.

The obstacles to implementing a program of treating borrowers according to their needs are varied.   One of the greatest difficulties lies in overcoming the faculty's attitude that they somehow are deserving of special consideration. If a faculty member believes that he belongs to an elite group, it may be impossible to convince him that people outside this special group are deserving of the same consideration.   Requiring him to show need when he never had to in the past demands an abrupt change in his ways of thinking.   Librarians must decide how best to meet this challenge and whether the effort is worth the end result.   Although privileges such as separate telephones can be easily denied or extended to other library users, librarians may be hesitant about instituting more severe measures such as limited borrowing or withdrawal of faculty participation in the book selection process. They may feel that faculty support is needed when the library staff approaches the college or university administration for money.   Faculty cooperation may be vital to the implementation of library programs such as bibliographic instruction. These beliefs may not be entirely realistic, but they are difficult to overcome.   Maintaining good public relations with everyone is not possible.   The ill feeling produced by withdrawing privileges from one group may be offset by the good will arising from another group receiving needed services.

Extending special services to everyone needing them encounters difficulties of another kind.   The demand may

far exceed the ability of the library to provide these services.
Space may not be available to accommodate all who request
it.   If no funds are available for additional staff and space,
a program can still be instituted based on existing conditions.
Guidelines can be established, staff reorganized if necessary,
and procedures rewritten.   Once new criteria and priorities
are established for the use of each service, the program is
no more difficult to administer than the one it replaces.   Although the demand for services may be greater than the supply, those receiving the services will obtain them on the basis
of their need and not solely because of their status.

A HARD LOOK AT RESERVE

by Norman D. Stevens

Many states and localities are now proposing to pass "sunset laws" under which government agencies would have to justify their existence on a periodic basis in order to receive continued funding. The theory behind these proposed laws is that too often programs are established to meet a specific need but continue to operate long after that need has been met or no longer exists. This concept may have only limited validity on a large scale. Certainly institutions of higher education and their libraries have, for the most part, already demonstrated their value over a period of time and ought not to have to justify their basic mission periodically. The concept may, however, have considerably greater validity if it is applied to specific programs within an institution. Perhaps it should be adopted by academic libraries as a means of examining and evaluating their programs on a periodic basis. Faced with a stringent review of this kind, the reserve system undoubtedly would be among those activities most hard pressed to justify their existence in almost any academic library.

In many academic libraries the circulation of reserve material is high, but such figures, taken alone, are not an adequate measure of effectiveness. The personal observation of many librarians and virtually every report in the literature serve to document the very real weaknesses of the reserve system. As early as 1940 Branscomb was decrying the waste involved in such systems. Downs noted that "students, librarians, and faculty members are in agreement that the reserve book plan is unsatisfactory."[1] Yet lacking the kind of review that a "sunset law" would demand, reserve systems are continued with no change. Instead we tinker with the mechanics by, for example, shifting from open to closed reserve systems. We may even turn to automation under the guise of improving the system.

All those involved have their own set of complaints.
Students either complain that the material assigned is not
placed on reserve promptly enough or that the faculty member pays no attention, either in class or on exams, to the
material that he has placed on reserve.   They may also complain, if in fact they actually attempt to use the system, about
the poor service and the long wait that may be involved in
locating material that turns out to be inconsequential.

The faculty are most likely to complain about the
amount of work the library expects them to do before material is placed on reserve and about how slow the library is
to place material on reserve.   They are also likely to pass
along a range of unsubstantiated student complaints about the
unavailability of material that is supposed to be on reserve.

Librarians complain that the faculty are consistently
late in making their requests, show no understanding of copyright restrictions that limit the number of photocopies of a
single article the library is able to make for reserve use,
and have placed on reserve excessive quantities of material
which students never even bother to look at.

Other complaints are also lodged.   Many feel that extensive use of reserve readings tends to restrict students to
the use of that material and discourages broader use of the
library.   A more recent criticism is that, since material
placed on reserve is likely to be in high demand, these systems tend to limit access to needed material by other users,
especially those who find material by browsing in the stacks.

The net result in most academic libraries is that the
reserve system is a source of frustration for all who have
to deal with it.   To make matters worse, it has little demon-
strable educational value and may, in fact, seriously hinder
the best use of library materials.

Reserve systems have been in existence since the late
1800s and may originally have been both useable and useful.
In providing specific access to a limited body of material
that all students in a relatively small class were required to
read within a given period of time, reserve systems generally
worked reasonably well.   With the advent of paperbacks,
photocopy machines, changes in teaching methods, and increases in class size, reserve systems, whose basic policies
and procedures have remained unchanged since they were first
established, have been asked to meet new needs that they were
not designed to, and cannot, handle.

Since it is no longer possible in any way to use the
reserve system for freshmen and sophomore courses that
may have enrollments of 500 or more students, faculty in
many institutions have abandoned its use for those courses.
They have been forced to find more imaginative solutions to
meet those needs.   Unfortunately, when they are faced with
enrollments for upper-class and even graduate courses of
sizes once common at the lower levels, many faculty have
tended to turn to the same system.   On the surface, the conditions seem to be the same.   They are, in reality, quite
different.   Required readings are more likely to be met at
those levels by the use of a combination of textbooks and
paperbacks.   The reserve system is asked to handle a quantity of material that all students may be expected to have
some supplementary acquaintance with or which only one or
two students in a course are expected to know in depth. Often
in these cases reserved books are used because the faculty
member views them as the only way to overcome the deficiencies of the library's circulation system, which may not
provide for the efficient recall of material.   The increase
in theft and mutilation has added to reserve's burden.   Often
it is also viewed, with some justification, as the only way
the library can be reasonably sure that the first student doing
an assignment will not steal the book or tear out the article.

In any case, the predictable result, which is amply
documented in the literature, is that a large percentage of
the material placed on reserve is never used at all and that
much of the remainder is used by only a few students.   It
is a waste of the faculty member's time to go through the
complicated procedures required to place material on reserve.
It is an even greater waste of the library's scarcest resource,
personnel, to put on reserve material that will never be used,
only to turn around and remove it a few months later.   It is
above all a waste of the students' time to require the one or
two who may actually use the material to do so under unnecessary restrictions.   Finally, it is a disservice to all other
users to remove from the shelves for no good reason material that they might wish to use.

If an academic library were forced to justify the continued existence of its reserve system under a "sunset law,"
what steps could be taken to alter and improve the system?
It might be possible to define initially a general statement of
purpose based on meeting a series of defined needs.   With
such a statement to guide them, the library staff could then
work with faculty and students to identify ways in which library materials needed for use in a specific course could be

made available to those students who need to use them, at
the time they need to, with maximum flexibility in time and
place.   Initially this would certainly take considerable professional time.   It might have to be done over a period of
several years, perhaps starting with those faculty who have
placed the most material on reserve or whose students have
made the least use of material on reserve.   It could be initiated simply by not responding to a request to place material
on reserve but by insisting on discussing in detail with the
faculty member his course and its relationship to library resources.   A series of interviews with students who have been
identified as heavy users of reserve also could be undertaken
to determine what their needs are for the kind of material
normally placed on reserve and how they feel those needs
might best be met.   Finally, the library staff involved in the
process could examine again in detail their policies and procedures with a view to making radical changes and not just
minor adjustments.

     Through such a process a number of alternatives
might be identified and pursued.   These might include: the
identification of a broader range and depth of library materials that might be appropriate for use in a specific course
and that might also lessen the competition for materials that
leads to theft and mutilation; the placing of fewer items on
reserve for shorter periods of time for specific assignments;
closer follow up on the use of material by both the faculty
and the library; the wider use of permanent noncirculating
basic collections that remain in the stacks; the purchase by
the library of more duplicate copies and subscriptions; the
development of circulation control policies and procedures,
especially automated ones, that provide for more flexibility
in the length of loan periods and the recall of material; and
the wider use, with the library taking an active role, of
commercial, and even locally developed, on-demand publication programs that enable books of supplementary readings
designed for a specific course to be produced and made available to students inexpensively.

     In any case it is clear that a major reform of the re-
serve system in academic libraries is badly needed.   In fact
it might not be too bad, except for the difficulties that it
would present to the students, if reserve systems in a few
institutions were abolished totally under a "sunset law" program.   It might well force all of us to take a more careful
look at the alternatives to what is one of our least useful
services.

Note

1. Robert B. Downs, Resources of Canadian Academic and Research Libraries (Ottawa: Association of Universities and Colleges of Canada, 1967), p. 84.

LIBRARIANS IN A TIME OF UNCERTAINTY

by Scott Bruntjen

It has become fashionable to talk about the uncertainty of funding for higher education. Those academic librarians in management positions who began their professional lives after the influx of federal money during the 1960s have had little experience with problems similar to the current crisis facing schools today: i.e., problems caused by extreme inflation, the recent decrease in state and federal funding, and the national projections for fewer students beginning in the late 1970s. Old timers in academic libraries point to the past cyclical nature of support, noting that when they first took their jobs there were "payless paydays" or nonexistent book budgets. "I've been through this before," they note. "The cycle will reverse." Perhaps it is time to question this optimism.

While at the outset it may seem that little has changed from the 1930s, 1940s or 1950s when it comes to the changing nature of financial support for higher education, there are differences, especially for the library. Inflation has shrunk the book buying power of the 1967 dollar to a mere 54 cents today. During the 25-year period from 1929 to 1954, inflation eroded a total of only 25 cents from the book dollar. Today, inflation is running almost <u>six times</u> that of the 1940s. [1]

Faculty friends of the library who, in the past, saw the library as the "heart of the campus" are now forced to compete with it for those few uncommitted dollars that remain after the salaries, benefits, and unavoidable operating expenses are paid. When it comes to selecting either faculty research support or an $800 journal subscription, the journal may well lose.

Such competition among would-be friends is bad enough, but the effect of the wholesale invasion of new curricula offered at off-campus locations during hours and days that are not

in the traditional college calendar invites all-out financial
warfare.   In the finance offices, where resource allocation
decisions affecting program continuance or demise are made,
it is increasingly clear that money, even in state-supported
institutions, comes from or because of students.   Students
come not for the traditional liberal arts, five-days-per-week
undergraduate offering at the main campus but, instead, for
Continuing Education Units in practical courses at convenient
locations and times.   The competition for the few uncommitted
funds brings about either support for new off-campus curricula
or for faculty research or for the book budget, or, more often, for an insufficient amount of each.

As the pressure mounts on financial officers to rebud-
get the few dollars that have materialized, areas of interest--
off-campus centers, the School of Business, and the library,
for example--are asked to submit justifications for their insufficient portions.   Here, it seems, is where the sharpest
deviation from the past occurs.   The off-campus centers with
their growing enrollments have an impact on total institutional
profits if they are not funded.   The School of Business, using
its expertise to present a multitude of plans, goals, consequences, and costs, convinces the funders that they have
thought through their programs, their productivity, their needs.
The library, however, finds itself in trouble, with its leadership unprepared for making the case for the library in this
highly constrained environment.   The financial officers know
the cost per credit hour by department, but all they know of
the library is cost.   Cost and more cost are recorded; yet
when the library is asked to substantiate its needs, when it
is asked to show the value it provides for the university,
nothing comparable to "credit-hour production" is provided
by the library manager.

This time the cycle is different.   Changes in allegi-
ances and curriculum, severe inflation, reduced total financial support, all on top of a multifold increase in information
needs, have created a new environment for the library manager.   Alleged productivity and performance measures such as
"gross, out-of-library circulation" or the "count of books
per student" may have been valid in a less pressured, more
certain time.   In this new library environment, the continued
use of such productivity measures has led librarians to provide that last item the financial officer needs: something to
give up.   Now the president and his public relations officers
can decry the effect that insufficient funding has on the campus: the library, that "vital" unit in the academic institution
cannot be supported this year.

Librarians do not recognize the new environment in which they live. Consider, for example, the continued use of circulation figures as a measure of the library's impact upon the academic community. The danger with such figures is that they can and do go down. When such indicators begin to drop, librarians tend to stick with the measure by dividing it by the number of students since, if that number is also down, the measure of circulation will look better. They may simply note the lack of a book budget adequate to provide new materials which will circulate; or, reaching for a blameworthy social problem, they may lament the impact of television on reading habits. The avoided explanation might be that the indicator of "out-of-library circulation" has become an obsolete measure. Perhaps all those business students are using financial looseleaf sources in the library rather than borrowing books.

It seems that a combination of factors has produced a new library operating environment that calls for skills not currently held by many library managers. In essence, librarians need to be able to reanalyze their fundamental decisions and restate their needs to financial decision makers in the language of the finance office. This is not as difficult as it might seem if one will question old assumptions, accept some of the basic tenets of decision analysis, and use some simple analytical techniques to reevaluate the library and its programs.

In a description of decision making, Keeney and Raiffa write that "it is almost a categorical truism that decision problems in the public domain are very complex. They almost universally involve multiple conflicting objectives, nebulous types of nonrepeatable uncertainties, costs and benefits accruing to various individuals, businesses, groups and other organizations (as well as) effects that linger over time and reverberate throughout the whole societal superstructure. It would be nice if we could feed the whole mess into a giant computer and program the superintellect to generate an 'objective correct' response. It just can't be done!"[2]

But there are some things librarians can do to sort out those areas that do need more formal analysis, to analyze those problems, and to present ideas and plans effectively. A sophisticated computer program termed the Venture Evaluation and Review Technique (VERT), which was first developed to manage multi-million dollar research and development projects for the Department of Defense, might be applicable to an analysis of collection development strategy and decisions.

VERT, a modification of PERT (Program Evaluation and Review Technique), permits the manager to construct several
trial chains of decisions to reach a desired group of outcomes.
VERT then simulates the project as it might behave in the
future under certain specified constraints and tells the manager what is likely and what is not likely to happen, when, and
with what costs.

A program that was designed to estimate costs, show
consequences of decisions, and measure effects of those decisions on future performance seems applicable to the examination of several library decisions under the uncertainties of
changing curricula and fund support. It is one thing to tell
the financial officer that $500,000 is needed because serial
costs are now over $300,000 and rising rapidly. It is another
to simulate different collection development strategies and to
forecast possible collection performance degradation or improvement in fiscal 1981, associated with a specific decision
to spend $400,000 in a ratio of three serials dollars to two
book dollars in 1978. The exact answer will not fall out,
but by employing a little "sensitivity analysis"--that is, seeing
how much one variable affects the final outcome by holding all
other factors constant--the manager can present different budget levels, different expenditure strategies, and can predict
different performance rates for tomorrow or five years from
now.

The National Center of Higher Education Management
Systems (NCHEMS), in a project unrelated to VERT, has developed a framework for and definitions of measures that describe what the library does and is capable of doing. [3]   A
library manager using the NCHEMS technique could evaluate
any major library asset. The collection, for example, could
be described by a cross tabulation of the number of items per
Library of Congress or Dewey category, with the number of
potential users arranged by Higher Education General Information Survey (HEGIS) categories. From this one would
know, for example, the number of history books per history
major. This measure of potential could be compared to the
actual inhouse and circulation use of the material. Thus one
could determine, in this example, how many history books
are used by patrons who have been grouped by HEGIS categories. Using this relationship of potential and actual performance, one might develop a collection performance measure which could indicate the effectiveness of past collection
development decisions and guide future purchases.

The matching of any method that provides a comprehensive structured look at the outcomes produced by the library, such as that of NCHEMS, with any method that attempts to forecast the impact of today's choices under various
future constraints, such as VERT, might help library decision
makers in the effective organization and presentation of the
library's needs.   It is those library decision makers who
must cope with a library environment that has thrown new
requirements, new competitors, and new power centers against
what is now one of the most vulnerable activities on campus.
The actual techniques discussed here are not important.   What
the library manager needs to recognize is that this new environment exists and that it requires new and more precise
analysis and expression of library needs.   Other areas can
switch to cheaper coal or remove every other light bulb to
save money.   They are rewarded for such actions.   There
are ways to save money in libraries, but in the long run the
goals of collection building and services imply spending money
creatively.   In this time of uncertainty, it takes a new approach to develop the strategy to support this creativity.

Notes

[1]American Library Annual for 1956-1957 (N. Y.:   R. R. Bowker, 1957), p. 91 and The Bowker Annual of Library and
Book Trade Information, 22d ed. (N. Y.:   R. R. Bowker,
1977), p. 335.
[2]Ralph L. Keeney and Howard Raiffa, Decisions with Multiple
Objectives: Preferences and Value Tradeoffs (N. Y.:   John
Wiley, 1976), p. 12.
[3]National Center for Higher Education Management Systems
at WICHE, Library Statistical Data Base; Commentary (Bould-
er, Colo.:   The Center, 1977).

INCREASING THE REFERENCE LIBRARIAN'S
PARTICIPATION IN THE RESEARCH PROCESS

by Kathleen Gunning

The information retrieval technology developed during the last decade has made an impact on the ways in which people do research. For example, commercial firms offering services such as current awareness updates on new research in a specific subject area and the sales of research articles make it possible for researchers to locate and procure information while bypassing the library. Confronted by these external capabilities, academic libraries need to reevaluate their roles as the principal access points for research materials. If the avowed mission of the library is to support the institution's research and teaching functions, the use of alternative organizations by the academic community should be a subject of careful analysis. We must ask ourselves whether librarians have indeed done as much as possible to assist in the process of research and teaching. Perhaps reference librarians can stimulate greater use of the library's resources and thus help to achieve the library's goal of being the main source of information on campus.

As a service organization, the library exists to meet the needs of its community. If these needs change over time and the library does not adapt to fulfill the new needs, especially during a period of economic uncertainty, it is in grave danger. Librarians who facilitate access to the collection have generally taken too passive a stance towards the contents of the collection. The active participation of librarians in bibliographic instruction and public relations programs is necessary but not sufficient. Reference librarians need to make an intellectual contribution by becoming involved not only in structures of research methodology but in understanding the intellectual content of the disciplines in which the research is done.

The reference department is the main interface between

the library's collections and its users.   Its primary task has
been to help the library user search for needed materials
more efficiently and comprehensively than he or she otherwise
could.   Reference librarians have used many methods, from
encounters at the card catalog to formal classroom instruction, in order to show beginning students and inadequately
trained faculty and advanced students how to use the library's
contents.   The reference librarian's opportunity to aid the
skilled researcher has often been limited to providing specific
pieces of information upon request.   Academic library staffs
have been too small to give extensive individual assistance to
each reader.   The computerized services that can compete
with libraries can also be brought into the library enabling
the librarian to increase the services offered to users at all
levels of competence.

      Even for the most experienced researcher, the task of
locating sources is tedious and time consuming.   If the research topic involves more than one discipline, many hours
must be spent in poring through the indexes of each field in
the hope of discovering the appropriate combination of subjects.   The advent of online bibliographic information retrieval
systems marks the beginning of new achievements in library
service.   The computer can combine the multiple subject
headings and/or other categories of information needed by the
researcher and print out a bibliography of the records in the
data base that fit these specifications.   This capability can
save the researcher enormous amounts of time and can provide more comprehensive searching than is possible manually.

      Reference librarians with expertise in both a subject
area and in information retrieval are of great help to researchers.   These librarians can see research problems in
terms of the current state of the discipline and can provide
information on the problem using the total array of online
and manual library services.

      In the course of their work, reference librarians could
also identify manual and online tools that are needed but not
available.   Librarians can work with nonprofit and commercial organizations to help provide these reference materials.
Joining with researchers who would benefit from specific
tools, librarians can seek the endorsement of appropriate
professional groups and library organizations for proposals
urging the creation of these reference works.   By thus dem-
onstrating that a market exists for these products, librarians
can make such proposals financially attractive to commercial

firms.   In this manner librarians can help to shape the forms
of bibliographic control for a subject area.

The appropriate level of expertise for reference staff
may vary among academic institutions.   Just as a library's
requirements for collection development in a subject field depend upon such factors as the specialization emphasized within that institution, the highest degree granted by the institution, and the relative importance of faculty teaching and research, so will the needs for public services subject special-
izations be governed by these considerations.   Probably only
the largest research institutions can contemplate a staff with
subject Ph.D.'s.   However, if an academic library hopes to
maintain its viability, staff members should be strongly urged
to upgrade their subject knowledge continuously through reading, classes, close contact with academic departments, or
degree programs.

Within the last few years even the largest libraries
have acknowledged the need to share materials.   As another
possible form of resource sharing, some mechanism could be
developed to provide libraries with access to subject specialists at other institutions.   The cost of training staff in information retrieval techniques and maintaining their skills is
high.   One solution to this problem would be to equip the entire staff with a basic understanding of machine-assisted reference, concentrating a few librarians in this area.   Institutions with fewer demands for such service could routinely
refer patron requests to libraries with this capability.   All
of these arrangements would channel the work done by the
faculty and students through the library rather than through
outside agencies.

If reference librarians will act decisively to make the
full range of information services plus specialized subject
competence available to the library user, then users will be
able to make fuller use of the library's collections, and the
image of the library will be enhanced.   We will be more
than mere custodians of the materials in the library.   We
will participate actively in the institution's research and
teaching functions.

A SIEGE OF COMMITTEES

by William D. Mathews

Not long ago I was at a committee meeting where the
chairman abruptly announced that the committee's work was
done and that the committee would therefore dissolve.   On
my way home I congratulated myself for being on a committee
that was sensible enough to self-destruct; and I tried to remember if this had ever happened to me before.   A few
weeks later, an agenda for yet another meeting of this same
committee appeared on my desk.   At first I thought it was a
mistake, but I should have known better.   The damned thing
was rising from the ashes to haunt me.   Someone had discovered some "unfinished business," and with this new purpose an additional round of meetings was called--another
committee with a life of its own, deadly but undying.

Academic libraries are being buried under an ava-
lanche of committees.   Some of the reasons are obvious.
The popularity of committees is due in part to the fact that
academic libraries are in academic institutions where committees are a favorite artillery piece of campus politicians.
Another reason why academic libraries are so pestered by
committees has to do with the increasing tendency of libraries
to join consortia, resource-sharing cooperatives, and networks, each of which means a new sphere of concerns, a
new relationship, and invariably new committees to join.
Still another reason for the proliferation of committees is
that they afford an all-too-easy way for managers to get
some work done on a problem for which they failed to budget or allocate resources.   Whatever the reason, this pro-
clivity to form committees is evidently here to stay.   If we
cannot eradicate committees, we can at least try to learn
to make them more efficient and to discover ways to manage
them better.

One factor that bears directly on the efficiency of a
committee is its size.   There is a well-known saying that

the best meetings are held by a committee of three when two
people can't make it.   This would qualify as an intimate committee by any standard.   Research on the subject shows that
the best size for a working committee is 4. 6 persons.   I
take this to mean that four persons work well together, and
sometimes five--not that fractional persons are to be sought.
The efficiency of a committee declines rapidly once eight or
more people participate.   New social dynamics come into
play, inhibiting the ready exchange of ideas.   Committee activity gets smothered under housekeeping chores and sinks
under the sheer weight of the formalities required to keep
the committee afloat.   There is a change in spirit and attitude; people who would otherwise speak up become silent.
Large committees often regroup into vocal minorities and
other factions--tendencies which are destructive of the essential committee process.   In the large committee there is invariably someone with an ax to grind, someone else who has
become catatonic or lapsed into a reverie, still others who
would rather not attend but can't afford to miss out on the
action.   Again, academic libraries are in the worst of worlds,
for not only are there too many committees but most of them
are of unwieldy size.

Yet it is the large committee that makes the strongest
demand on our management abilities.   To get a large committee to act, all its members must be mentally in the same
place at the same time.   The likelihood that this will happen
spontaneously and without guidance is as remote as the likelihood that a road race with as many people would end in a
dead heat.   Without persuasion and coaxing, the committee
will never come together.   Usually it is assumed that the
chair brings the necessary guiding force to bear; but in a
large committee this is not always possible.   If we break
down the various committee management functions and look
at them separately, it becomes apparent that the chair might
not be able to handle them all.

I would like to take the view that a committee is a
specialized structure designed to allow people to exchange
ideas under constraints of time.   This is not so much meant
to be a definition of a committee as a description of its dimensions.   A conference, for example, could be similarly
described.   I wish, though, to use this description to point
up the basic social nature of committees and to point out that
if we begin to see committees as a delicate balance of people,
ideas, and time, we can understand more easily some of the
problems and pitfalls in managing a committee adequately.

Following on this concept of the committee as a complex of
people, ideas, and time, I would like to postulate a framework for coping with committees built around a consideration
of three specific committee management functionaries--the
time-keeper, the idea-keeper, and the people-keeper.

The time-keeper monitors and manages the time budget of the committee, establishes a time perspective, and
maintains a sense of proportion between the importance of an
item being considered and the time used to work on it.   The
time-keeper should have some control over arranging the
agenda to ensure that urgent items are not buried by inconsequential ones.   It is the time-keeper's responsibility to see
that time is not squandered on the ridiculous.   The time-
keeper also guards against two time-related blunders that
committees often make when dealing with important decisions.
The first of these is a panic reaction or a "rush to judgment."
This counter-productive mode is induced by the perception
(usually unrealistic) that there is insufficient time to thoroughly analyze alternatives.   Some action must be taken even if
it isn't the best.   The other time-related blunder is the
opposite--procrastination.   There the committee comes to
believe that time is of little consequence, that time will alter
the importance of the decision, or, perhaps, that time will
change the ground rules, making a decision unnecessary.

The time-keeper senses that committee processes have
a life cycle: problems are resolved through discovery, discussion refinement, understanding, review, and decision.
The time-keeper perceives these inherent patterns of dealing
with topics and meters the committee's time accordingly.
Finally, the time-keeper can detect fatigue, ennui, or ma-
laise, and knows when to call for a coffee break.   Occasionally, the time-keeper will deftly call for a break when it is
clear that progress is being impeded by the formal structure
of the committee itself.   A break allows for the informal
caucusing, private exchanges, and realignments of support
that are sometimes needed to move the committee forward.

The idea-keeper is ideologically inclined and understands what the meeting is supposed to accomplish.   The
idea-keeper controls the agenda, injects a sense of purpose,
keeps the committee on track, remarks on progress and decisions as they are made.   The idea-keeper nurtures the development of an idea, knows when it's ripe for picking, savors
subtle nuances, and can often improve on or restate thoughts
more articulately than the originator of an idea.   The idea-

keeper knows when to obtain wider points of view, close off
a discussion, or ask for a vote.   The idea-keeper guards
against collective sensory overload and ensures that the committee does not take up more problems than it can handle effectively.   The idea-keeper is also responsible for framing
the work statement, charge, or charter of the committee.
However brief such a statement may be, no committee should
be without one.   A strong test of the idea-keeper's ability is
to see if the idea-keeper can write, in general terms, the
minutes of a meeting before the meeting takes place.

The people-keeper is a kind of master of ceremonies
and protocol, and is socially adept.   This person is sensitive
to the need of each committee member to feel wanted and
useful.   The people-keeper encourages everyone to participate
in deliberations and is completely nonjudgmental about the
individual contributions.   The people-keeper sees to it that
people are introduced to each other and conveys a sense of
unity and warmth.   The people-keeper also arranges for the
meetings to be held in comfortable surroundings, free of dis-
tractions and interruptions.   If one member of the committee
becomes obstreperous and attacks another, the people-keeper
pours oil on the troubled waters by conveying a positive mood
which lowers tempers and further contributes to the feeling
of togetherness and singularity of purpose.

A strong chairman might be able to encompass all
three of these committee management functions but more often
will find it useful, especially in larger committees, to dele-
gate one or more of them.   The social and nonjudgmental
role of the people-keeper frequently runs counter to the astute
cunning of the idea-keeper.   The time-keeper's desire to
move the committee forward may be at cross-purposes to
both the idea-keeper's desire to crystallize a thought or the
people-keeper's wish to hear all points of view.

In any event, committee chairmanship and management
must be a strong and conscious effort.   A committee may
well be a social structure, but it is by no means a democratic
one.   Any chairman who thinks that a committee can run itself without leadership deserves the ultimate surprise in a
hidden agenda item called "appointing a new chair. " If academic librarians can't fight the endless procession of committees, at least they should try to contain the damage by limiting their size.   In any case, better management techniques
are long overdue, for a mismanaged committee is a blizzard
of words.

ACADEMIC LIBRARIAN:
LIBRARIAN OR FACULTY MEMBER?

by Louise S. Sherby

Too many academic librarians concern themselves with
nothing more than answering the immediate reference question
or cataloging a particular book. This is not to imply that
these are not important tasks, but if academic librarians
want to be recognized as professionals and faculty members,
then that is not enough. Academic librarians must recognize
the additional responsibilities of faculty beyond classroom
teaching and at the same time realize that active participation
in professional activities will enhance not only their role as
librarians, but also provide opportunities for personal growth
and development. Librarians cannot isolate themselves; they
must become active and visible members of the community in
which they work if they are to continue to demand faculty
status.

Faculty status is desired in most instances by academic librarians primarily to equalize their salaries and benefits
with those of the "teaching" faculty. A second reason for
wanting faculty status is to enable librarians to become part
of the faculty, traditionally the group on campus with considerable input into the governance of the institution. There may
be other real benefits, too, such as representation on the
college or university's governing body (the Faculty Senate or
Council), eligibility for tenure and leaves, or possible recognition as an academic department that has an important educational and teaching role to play within the goals of the institution. All of these benefits are, of course, positive things
which enhance the librarian and his role in the academic community.

However, faculty status also carries with it implicit
responsibilities that are not mutually exclusive with those of
the academic librarian; rather they often complement each
other. Certainly high standards of service are among the

most important goals for both librarians and faculty. Scholarly interests such as research, writing, and continuing education are equally important. In addition, participation in
professional library activities needs to be considered, such
as memberships, committee assignments, or offices in local
state and national organizations and participation in college
and university affairs both within the library and campus-
wide. These activities provide essential channels for the
kind of personal and professional growth and development
that must take place if librarians or faculty members are to
provide effective service throughout their careers. How can
these kinds of activities and interests not reflect well on both
the librarians' on-the-job performance and their acceptance
as faculty colleagues by the "teaching" faculty? If more
academic librarians participated seriously in at least one or
more of the above activities, then perhaps academic librarians would be accepted more readily as valued members of
the faculty by their colleagues. How can librarians expect
to be treated as important participants in the educational
process when many, by a lack of concern with and participation in activities related to the library, the institution, and
librarianship demonstrate a serious lack of professionalism?

Library administrators, too, need to recognize the
importance of staff participation on college and university
committees, at professional meetings, and in research and
continuing education activities. They should provide time,
office space, and funds to allow staff members the opportunity to participate in these activities effectively. Too often
staff members are made to feel that they are not allowed to
leave the library--whether this is in fact true or not. But
it is absolutely necessary for librarians to be recognized as
members of the academic community who not only pull their
own weight but can make worthwhile and valuable contributions.

One of the major problems administrators may face
after encouraging their staff to participate in these activities
is to find someone to work in the library while everyone else
is attending meetings or doing research. This can be a serious problem to which there is no easy answer. It is a situation that calls for much cooperation among all members of
the library staff and administration. One needs to remember,
too, that there may be specific criteria used in evaluating the
faculty that reflect participation in these activities. This can
be especially true for those librarians in faculty unions. Released time for study, and other such considerations, are
often spelled out in collective bargaining contracts. Perhaps

consideration of flexible scheduling and similar adjustments
can help ease the situation. A redefinition of job responsibilities or a reduced work load may also be called for. One
word of caution, however: it is unrealistic to expect staff
members to work full time in the library and participate in
all of these other activities on their own time. Expecting
this can often lead to serious morale problems and a constant
turnover of staff. Both the administration and the staff have
to work together to find better ways to utilize everyone's
time--staff's and administrator's. Those who respond in a
positive manner to this challenge can do both effectively.

What about librarians who opt out and do not wish to
or are unable to participate in these professional activities?
Over the length of their careers they will not be able to
function effectively and will be less able to hide this as poor
faculty members often can. They will likely find they are
passed over for promotions, denied tenure, or not reappointed
when the annual decisions must be made. They will also be
subjected to possible peer-group pressure similar to that of
"keeping up with the Joneses." Another probability is that
they will not be consulted by either their peers or the administration when important decisions have to be made.

For librarians at the other extreme, their job performance may suffer. They may advance too rapidly, and they
may also be subjected to peer-group pressures of another
kind.

Unconsciously, they may be setting up a race in which
other library faculty feel compelled to compete at an impossible rate, and attempts may be made to slow down the whirlwind. Between these two extremes, there is ample opportunity for increased participation in professional activities without detriment to library service.

If academic librarians would recognize their role as
one of real worth, then perhaps a true professional attitude
toward the field of librarianship could develop naturally.
There would no longer be a question of "librarians or faculty members"; rather they would be recognized as valued and
valuable faculty colleagues who happen to be librarians.

ESSAYS FROM THE SEMINAR

INTRODUCTION

The original proposal for the New England Academic Librarians' Writing Seminar emphasized the fact that each participant would be expected to write a book-length essay on some aspect of library cooperation. In two respects that presented problems. First, because the final number of applicants was more limited than had been expected, it was not feasible to use the possible topic for a longer essay as one of the selection criteria. Consequently, while each of the participants selected had indicated an interest in writing on some aspect of library cooperation, it soon became apparent that that was neither feasible or desirable. Each had other more immediate interests and, of course, those interests changed over the life of the Seminar, especially in the case of those participants who changed jobs. Successful writing most often comes from immediate interests and, thus, early on in the Seminar it was agreed that each participant would be free to write a longer essay on any topic of particular interest to her or him. What is presented here, then, is a series of essays on a number of disparate topics reflecting the interests, experiences, and work situations of the members of the Seminar. The coherence of theme that I had hoped to achieve is not present but I do not believe that that in any way distracts from the value of the Seminar or the quality of the work that is presented here.

The second problem was, in most respects, a far more serious one. It was simply that I may have been too ambitious in outlining the requirements of the Seminar. The jump from writing a short essay for a professional journal to writing a full-length book essay is a big one. In retrospect it can be suggested that it might have been better to have the second mandatory project be the writing of a longer article designed for publication in a professional journal. Had more of the participants had previous writing experience, this probably would not have been such a stumbling block. As it was, the writing of these longer pieces required a great deal of time and effort on the part of each of the participants.   In addition, it was not always possible to treat each of these longer pieces with as much care and attention within the Seminar as it had been with the shorter essays.   Here again pieces of an intermediate length might have been more satisfactory.   It was largely the effort required by the participants in completing these longer essays that delayed the final completion of the total project by just under a year. On the whole, however, I believe that the experience of doing the longer pieces has been a good one and should enable us to be better equipped and better able to deal with the writing of shorter journal articles.

These essays require no individual introductions.   Each speaks for itself and should be treated as a separate entity. Each does represent the expenditure of a considerable amount of time and effort on the part of the writer and each, I can assure the reader, represents a significant improvement over the initial drafts in every respect.   In that regard the Seminar accomplished a good deal.

Norman D. Stevens

MAKING DO WITH LESS:
A PROBLEM WITH A PARTIAL SOLUTION

by Scott Bruntjen

Abstract

With fiscal constraints on libraries becoming more severe and more permanent, planning on making do with less becomes more critical. Better management information, even though the availability of such information may increase the risk for library managers, is essential. This paper describes a series of library information gathering devices developed by the National Center for Higher Education Management Systems and how they might be used to improve library performance and the use of library resources. Finally, the need for some coordinated approach to library management information systems is briefly outlined.

INTRODUCTION

As the title implies, this paper, more than lamenting the current lack of resource support for libraries, will also begin to suggest a way out of the problems imposed by the stringent financial conditions which began to affect libraries in the 1970s.

The times of limited resources will not disappear in the next year or two. It is just as certain that this new environment calls for creative management of the few dollar and staff resources that remain.

In the early attempts to cope with the new environment librarians came to realize that resources would no longer continue to expand. Their reaction was one of unplanned and often irrational cutbacks. In a few cases such an approach turned out to be beneficial, but as an overall strategy these

kinds of cuts could not be continued indefinitely.   After the
shock over the loss of relatively unlimited resources wore
off, library managers realized that they needed information
about the library if they were to meet the financial crisis in
a planned way.

Unfortunately, the traditional information gathering
systems that were available for librarians did not produce
data for decision making.   One knew something about the
size of the resources available in libraries but little about
how the resources were allocated.   Even less was known
about what was produced because of this allocation.   Predict-
ing probable library performance levels in the future in light
of the current patterns of expenditures was more difficult.

What has been identified here as a management information void begins to highlight a highly complex area of inquiry.   The bulk of this essay is oriented toward suggesting
a plan to fill that information gap.   The system presented in
this paper will not provide all of the solutions to all of the
problems that librarians will face in the 1980s and perhaps
beyond.   This work was supported by the Pennsylvania State
College Educational Services Trust Fund and the Visiting
Scholar Program of the National Center for Higher Education
Management Systems.   What this suggested information gathering system will provide is a method of conceptualizing the
programmatic activities of the library.   Through the use of
a system such as this, librarians will be able to determine
what is produced with a particular resource expenditure pattern, and thus should be able to anticipate problem areas
before they cause an irrevocable expenditure of highly limited
dollar and time resources.   The system suggested is a tool
to aid in decision making.   It is not a panacea.   It may not
maximize resource use, but it should help.

It seems strange that librarians should be in the position of lacking information but when it comes to management
decisions we are.   What is needed is a realization that the
economic problem is serious and that it will continue, and a
method to begin to fill this information void that librarians face.

THE LIBRARY ENVIRONMENT IN THE LATE 1970S

A Time of Limited Resources

The basic resource which keeps libraries healthy is

money, and money is much more difficult to come by today
than it used to be. In academic libraries this shortage may
manifest itself in a variety of ways. Outside funders may
limit the total dollar resource. Expenditures by categories,
such as for staff or for materials, may be individually controlled by funders located outside of the library. Transfers
among expenditure categories may not be permitted. The release of funds may be time-phased by month or quarter.
Funds may be limited to expenditure within one fiscal year.
The total number of staff may be constrained regardless of
the amount of money available. No matter how it is presented, money today is limited, restricted, constrained, difficult
to acquire, or just plain "tight."

A discussion about the reasons why monetary restrictions exist would lead to discussions of social conditions, national economics, oil embargoes, and the like. None of these
topics is germane here but, for planning purposes, there are
some conditions that go along with "tight" money that need to
be mentioned. Not only is the total available dollar resource
difficult to expand but an examination of the Consumer Price
Index clearly illustrates the fact that the same size resource
continues to shrink in buying power. The 1954 library materials dollar was able to purchase more than 75% of what
it could in 1929, yet in 1977 that same materials dollar could
purchase only half of what it could in 1967. Roughly speak-
ing, inflation in library purchases is running ahead of general
inflation. The current library inflation rate is almost six
times the library inflation rate of 30 years ago. For planning
purposes, therefore, even a ten per cent annual growth in the
library materials budget is, in reality, a loss in purchasing
power. [1]

In the 1959 and again in the 1975 ACRL Standards for
College Libraries it is suggested that the library should receive about six per cent of the institution's "educational and
general expenditures." Surveys show that this level of support is not available for academic libraries. An analysis of
national data from the Higher Education General Information
Survey (HEGIS) and from the Library General Information
Survey (LIBGIS) showed that, rather than that ACRL suggested
six per cent figure, academic libraries receive only an average of 4.3%. Using those figures, support for academic libraries is almost one-half a billion dollars a year short, on
a national level, of the minimum standard.

It becomes obvious that the ability to achieve a real

gain in the materials budget is probably impossible unless
large grants are received or unless the library staff is cut.
Unfortunately, or fortunately, depending upon one's perspective, even the option of cutting staff is often not available to
the library manager for, in many cases, staff is treated as
an institutional fixed expense while only funds for materials
purchases are considered discretionary and, thus, available
for reduction.

Inflation erodes the purchasing power of the library
dollar while limiting funds available to the entire institution,
but it is not the only cause for constrained resources in the
library. Institutions have looked to the immediate future of
the 1980s and have projected, to their dismay, that the potential number of "traditional students" will decrease. At the
same time the curriculum needs of current and future students
are radically different from those students of the past. The
fields in which some institutions have concentrated--teacher
education or the liberal arts, for example--have become so
satiated that students, heeding the guidance counselors' advice and seemingly driven by the desire for post-college employment, have demanded new programs. Colleges and universities have responded to those pressures.

For the library this rapid change in curriculum emphasis further constrains the resources while making future
planning almost impossible. Where does the money come
from to build a business administration collection? Who pays
to retrain the librarians who now must know about annual
reports and current operating ratios rather than about medie-
val manuscripts? How does one mollify the entrenched faculty power in the humanities when their materials allocation is
reduced?

To make matters even more difficult, institutions have
found that to attract students they will have to move outside
the traditional patterns of delivering education. The off-campus
center and the traveling professor teaching in the local community center fifty miles from the campus have become an
important part of the new delivery system. How does the
library support such operations? If the same course with
the same required reading list is taught at five scattered
sites, the pressure to buy duplicates increases. If the library
reneges on its commitment to those off-campus students it
may well find itself without much student or faculty support;
but if it attempts to provide materials for those off-campus
sites, it will find its budget even more pressured.

Even if the growth in recorded knowledge were slow this lack of funds would be a problem, but with the expansion both in information and in the means of presentation and retrieval of that information, the funding pressures increase.

To abrogate any of these responsibilities of the campus information center, however, may lead to funds being provided to those agencies, be they independent departmental libraries or the computer center, which are able to take on these functions.

Early Attempts to Cope with the New Environment

With the cutback in support received by libraries the basic assumption upon which the total library planning and management system had been constructed crashed.   This assumption was, simply, that resources would continue to expand.   In resource terms, what had been almost an open system became a closed system in which expenditures in any portion of the system limited growth in any other portion. The commitment to a new program required a reduction of effort elsewhere.   While often the same performance standard could be maintained for a time with fewer resources because of increased efficiency, there was a definite limit to the increases in efficiency and productivity that could be brought about.

Most library managers intuitively seemed to see the value of the efficiency route and they applied it with a vengeance.   Serials were cut; automated catalog support systems were implemented; overdue notices that used to number four or five were cut to one; hours were shortened.   In almost every case, however, all basic programs remained.   After the "fat" disappeared managers retained the same strategy, but now they pared past efficiency.   First it was "deferred maintenance" or equipment budgets of zero.   Initially there was little consequence but then performance rates began to suffer.   Several ploys were attempted: cut the service that will hurt the user so that political support for the beleaguered library will be generated, or, alternatively, cut the activities that are not directly seen so that waves will not be made. In either case there was little effort to determine how the continued provision of one service affected the ability to offer all others.   There was little work on the basic question of priorities; little work on determining the allocation of costs by function; little work on the whole issue that with limited

resources not everything could continue at the same rate forever.

The crisis that libraries began to face involved the
present and the future, but for the most part only portions of
the present, and almost none of the future, were recognized.
What seemed to go completely untouched was the fact that the
future performance of the organization is almost totally dependent upon the present as long as resources continue to be
extremely limited.

The basic tradeoff that seems best to highlight the
problem is the tension that exists between current staffing
levels and future collection performance.   Just the idea that
any tradeoff exists is repugnant to some librarians.   The fact
is that, because of the conditions identified earlier, if one
wants to build a collection that serves today and presents the
base for tomorrow, then there will have to be a decrease
somewhere else in the present budget.   To develop enough
capital for that kind of collection effort the cut will probably
have to be in the current personnel budget.   There is, in
such a situation, no single correct answer but there are a
host of wrong ones which are to be recognized and, it is
hoped, avoided.

A More Rational Approach

In the operation of libraries the first aspect of dealing
with the present and the future within the environment of constrained resources is to develop the attitude that, while without a doubt it will take energy, one must attempt to determine the present condition of the library and its probable
state in the next few years if present policies are followed.
This simple statement presents what appears to be an almost
insurmountable problem in conceptualization.   The tendency
is either to develop something highly complex and detailed,
which cannot be manipulated and which takes tremendous resources just to maintain, or, conversely, to gather such
simplistic data that they are not capable of modeling the real
world with enough precision to be useful.   What usually happens is that hundreds of individual counts are made and these
"statistics" are then collected.   The librarian may know the
number of directional questions answered but because there
is no coordinated data collection plan, few definitions to describe the data elements themselves, and no plan for analyzing the data, this management information effort usually does
not lead to, or support, planning.

The measurement of the "performance" of the library
is an even more difficult problem than the picturing of the
expenditure of library resources. It is an effort that must
be accomplished. The identification of the allocation of resources by function within a library is a necessary exercise
but, by itself, it is almost meaningless. Even if the allocation decisions of all libraries in the United States were compared, that information would tell us little. Suppose that all
libraries of a certain type everywhere allocated 60 per cent
of their dollar resources to personnel. The only response
that there could be to this fact is "so what?" What needs to
be connected to specific allocations is some measure of organization performance, and that performance has to be measured in terms of the individual institution's goals. If one library were to allocate 90 per cent of its budget to personnel
and a second were to allocate 90 per cent to collections, and
if their performance rates both equalled 100 per cent, one
could say that in the near future at least these two libraries,
based on their goals, had made good decisions. As must be
obvious, either, or both, of these libraries would probably be
in serious trouble if the long-range aspects of their allocation
decisions were examined.

While activity levels (i. e. , number of books circulated,
number of reference questions answered, etc.) do serve a
useful purpose, and while comparative data among libraries
of the same type may provide norms to aid in the initial allocation decisions, it is only by looking at a performance
"meter" that one can determine if a new allocation decision
is better than the old one, and then only for a specific library. Assuming that performance rates can be precisely
defined and calibrated so that a performance rate of 90 per
cent means the same thing everywhere, then this meter can
be used to monitor decisions made for the present or for the
future.

In looking at a management information system that
provides the library manager with the ability to make considered decisions, and to leave the realm of the "business
as usual" strategy, an immediate problem surfaces. It is
hoped that this ability to measure the present and to forecast
the future will provide information that may tempt one to
change present resource allocation policies, but such an action puts the decision maker in the position of high risk.
Knowing a little about what might happen may be worse than
knowing nothing about it. The implementation of such a management information system cannot be taken lightly. Instead,

it must be combined with an acceptance of an attitude that if the information says "act," the operators and managers of the library will consider the system's advice.

In an unconstrained resource environment there will be few risks to face, since any action can be accommodated and failure be corrected through the commitment of more dollars. Uncertainty and limits pose more difficult problems. While it takes a creative mind to design a specific program, it is much simpler to accomplish that task in an environment in which any reasonable resource request can be satisfied and in which that resource request does not by necessity destroy other programs. When one must be creative in the solution of program problems and must also realize that, because of limited resources, the implementation of one program requires the end of another program, then the manager may well be put in the high-risk position of deciding to limit, or terminate, a successful current program so as to shift resources to support a future need which may never pay off.

An example of this dilemma may be helpful. Assume that the time is 1970. As the acquisitions librarian you are building a collection to support a college that has a high number of teacher education majors. From rumor you find that the emphasis in curriculum may have to change if this college is to be successful in maintaining its overall enrollment. The materials budget is adequate for maintenance but it does not leave room for experimentation. You determine that it is likely that the new emphasis in the next few years may be business administration, although no one will make this prediction official. What do you do?

If you continue to support teacher education the current power structure will be satisfied; current users will be served; and for the present all will be acceptable. In the future, however, a catastrophic breakdown may occur if there is indeed a large change in curriculum emphasis. If you direct resources from teacher education materials to the basics for business administration, and if that shift does come about, the present users may suffer but the future ability of the collection to meet user needs will be maximized. Of course the shift may not take place, and if you support business administration in lieu of teacher education no one will be served. Here are all the components operating together. To make this decision you need to know the present allocation of resources with an evaluation through performance. You need to be able to project future performance of this same allocation strategy and competing strategies in several environments. You need to be willing to accept the risk inherent in change, especially where that change will cause a definite short-run degrading of performance with no certain future payoff.   Thus to accept a management information system is not a decision to be made lightly, for it may, by providing information, make the management job more difficult, rather than less.

There is a warning that needs to be expressed before a solution can be found for this need to develop and accept information about the present and the future.   It is, simply, that the data-gathering and analysis effort cannot be made so great that nothing happens in the library except data gathering and analysis.   What is not desired is the perfect model that cannot be implemented because if it were, all resources would be consumed in the information collection effort, or because it could never be completely developed.   A solution to the information problems that library managers face will be presented here with the understanding that it is not perfect, but that it is close enough to be useful and affordable.

MANAGEMENT INFORMATION: ALLOCATION AND PERFORMANCE

Developing Resource Allocation Information

Enter or leave a library and you are, in all probability, counted.   Check out a book or ask a reference question and somewhere these transactions become part of some data base.   Ask for a new book, an interlibrary loan, or a magazine and somewhere someone makes a mark on a scratch pad that by the end of the year has become a measure of something about that library and its ability to serve its users. Yet ask people who make those marks why they do it, or ask what happens to the information, and most often there is no answer.   What is lacking in management information in libraries is not the mass of individual statistics but a coordinated plan for the collection of information and a specific plan for the use of the information once it is accumulated.

In 1976 the National Center for Higher Education Management Systems (NCHEMS) began the "Library Statistical Data Base project"[2] (LSDB) in an attempt to provide a tool for library managers to use in planning and evaluation.   This project, which formed much of the philosophical and technical base for the Handbook of Standard Terminology and Guide to

Recording and Reporting Information About Libraries (Handbook) and for the Glossary of Standard Terminology for Libraries, Learning Resource and Media Centers (Glossary),
provides a framework for the collection and analysis of library management information.

        To understand both the problems inherent in looking
at a library and the power developed by this plan for data
collection and analysis as presented in the Handbook one needs
to envision the types of questions that the library manager
may want answered.   Consider the following area of interest:
"How many and what types of human resources do I have at
my disposal?   How can I describe these human resources?
How do I use these human resources?"

        Before such questions can be answered certain condi-
tions must be met and certain rules followed.   Ask such a
group of questions of more than one person and at least two
definitions for every data element would be used.   Clearly,
to make such a system work, especially if it is to develop
information that can be compared among several libraries,
a standard set of terminology is required.   The Glossary,
which provides these standard definitions, derives from the
work done for the library statistical data base as well as
from several ALA publications, from research in the field
of library performance measures, from work on national and
international standards for library statistics, and from the
work of National Center for Education Statistics (NCES) in
the LIBGIS program.

        If one were interested in the data element "Personnel
Resources, " for example, the description of that item could
be found in the Glossary.   In the case of Personnel Resources
six standard categories are provided.   Each of these six categories is further categorized and defined.   If one were interested in "Subject Specialists" it would be noted that they
are part of category three of Personnel Resources and, specifically, are "Specialists/Librarian Professionals. "   Within
this sub-category a Subject Specialist is "an exempt employee
who has academic preparation in a subject field or language,
usually beyond a Bachelor's degree, and is employed in collection development, specialized reference services and/or
bibliographic services in his/her field. "   Those who are not
used to the term "exempt employee" will find it defined elsewhere in the Glossary.

        After the establishment of a standard language, the

next criterion for a successful information system is a design
which encourages multiple use of the information collected.
If, for example, one were required to report on the Library
General Information Survey to NCES the number of "full time
male librarians, other than the chief librarian,"[3] then one
would not want to have to count this resource again in a different manner for internal use.   The general rule should be
that outside reporting requirements, which include federal
and state requirements as well as those of associations and
accrediting agencies, should be compatible with information
used internally.

Given that the information which is collected is comparable among libraries, and given that the reporting requirements of all outside agencies are coordinated and can be developed from the internal collection effort, then one only needs
to collect that information which answers the allocation and
planning considerations that are important to the particular
library.   This begins, probably, with the minimum set of
data that are required by outside agencies.

Continuing with the example of subject specialists, one
needs to be interested in these personnel as a component of
the broad category of human resources.   This specific asset
needs to be described in a manner that will give the manager
an idea of the price, quantity, and quality of the group as
well as a general demographic description.   Having looked at
the numbers and types of human resources available, one
next needs to ask how these subject bibliographers are utilized
at present.   By comparing the appropriate level of programmatic activity with the measures of personnel one should be
able to determine how and where these personnel are used.
By mapping the allocation of the combination of revenue, personnel, and facilities by function against activities one has a
picture of what happens, given this particular pattern of allocation.

By using this system a new manager, or the current
one who has never approached this problem before, can answer outside queries without too much effort but, more important, he or she can determine the library's environment,
have a description of its resources and the current allocation
of those resources by program, and display the activities that
the allocation produces.

Figure 1 presents the basic organization of the data
base.   In some smaller libraries the "programmatic activities,"

or the functions of the library, may well be expressed by Figure 1. In larger and more complex organizations more detailed data may be required. Figure 2 illustrates the various levels of disaggregation that can be accomplished by the use of this system. Users of the current Handbook will note that both Figures 1 and 2 have gone through several stages of development since the Data Base project began, yet, while the list of data elements that can be collected has been modified, these two simple illustrations still provide the basic philosophy of the system. In essence, Figure 1, with the programmatic activities expanded for larger libraries in Figure 2, presents all of the basic data elements that one would need to know to analyze a library.

For additional information the reader is directed to the Commentary to the Library Statistical Data Base (Commentary). If, after reading the Commentary, the reader would like to use the suggested approach, the forms and general plan for the collection of the information are available in a companion volume to the Commentary titled Library Statistical Data Base: Formats and Definitions (Formats and Definitions).

A further comment on Figures 1 and 2 is necessary. The library environmental data of Figure 1 place a library in its context, while the resources information presents what a library has available to perform its mission. These environmental and resource questions are much like the questions that one usually asks. How big is the library? What types of people does it serve? The program data, however, are somewhat different. They describe what a library does. What the program data portion of Figure 1 means is that data base system collects and provides the raw material for the analysis of the resource allocation strategies that the library manager has either made or is considering. Thus, in the box defined as "Personnel Measures of Cultural, Educational and Information Services," for example, will be questions in the data base that determine what level of person by training and education qualification is allocated to SDI Services. In the "Financial Measures of Cultural, Educational and Information Services" box are questions that, in part, determine how much such staff cost. By comparing the data collected through these questions, either in dollar terms or in percentage of budget terms or in percentage of staff available terms, with the same information developed for Technical Services an administrator can determine the present resource allocation strategy that is in place. In the Activity

(cont'd. on p. 72)

Figure 1

SUMMARY OF INFORMATION STRUCTURE FOR LIBRARIES

Organizational Goals and Objectives

ENVIRONMENTAL DATA
- External Setting
- Internal Organization
- Target Group

RESOURCE DATA
- Collection Resources
- Financial Resources
- Personnel Resources
- Facility Resources

PROGRAM DATA

Categories of Measures / Programmatic Functions	RESOURCE UTILIZATION MEASURES					
	Financial Measures	Personnel Measures	Facility Measures	Activity Measures	User Measures	Outcome/Performance Measures
Cultural, Educational, and Information Services						
Resource Distribution Services						
Collection Development Services						
Technical Services						
Administrative Services						

Figure 2

LEVELS OF PROGRAMMATIC ACTIVITIES

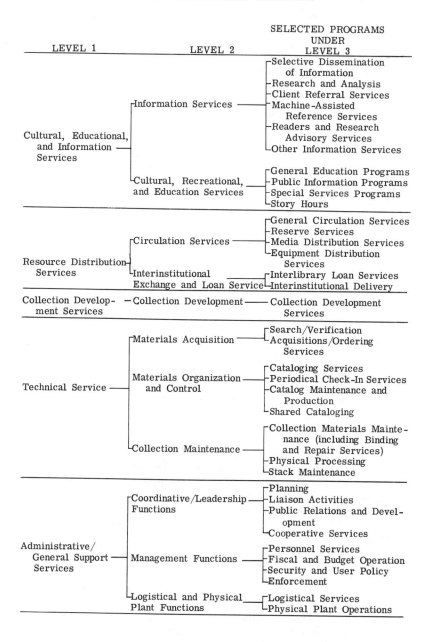

LEVEL 1	LEVEL 2	SELECTED PROGRAMS UNDER LEVEL 3
Cultural, Educational, and Information Services	Information Services	Selective Dissemination of Information Research and Analysis Client Referral Services Machine-Assisted Reference Services Readers and Research Advisory Services Other Information Services
	Cultural, Recreational, and Education Services	General Education Programs Public Information Programs Special Services Programs Story Hours
Resource Distribution Services	Circulation Services	General Circulation Services Reserve Services Media Distribution Services Equipment Distribution Services
	Interinstitutional Exchange and Loan Service	Interlibrary Loan Services Interinstitutional Delivery
Collection Development Services	Collection Development	Collection Development Services
Technical Service	Materials Acquisition	Search/Verification Acquisitions/Ordering Services
	Materials Organization and Control	Cataloging Services Periodical Check-In Services Catalog Maintenance and Production Shared Cataloging
	Collection Maintenance	Collection Materials Maintenance (including Binding and Repair Services) Physical Processing Stack Maintenance
Administrative/ General Support Services	Coordinative/Leadership Functions	Planning Liaison Activities Public Relations and Development Cooperative Services
	Management Functions	Personnel Services Fiscal and Budget Operation Security and User Policy Enforcement
	Logistical and Physical Plant Functions	Logistical Services Physical Plant Operations

Measures boxes are found questions that attempt to find the answer to what is done, given this expenditure of resources.

Figure 1 is the conceptualization of the entire data base. It defines the types of questions that are asked and the pieces of information that are developed by the system. By studying the cross tabulations that are possible one can begin to visualize the questions that can be answered and the comparisons that can be made.

Figure 2 illustrates the fact that the information developed by the data base can be provided at several levels of detail. In Administrative/General Support Services, for example, one may wish to know the total number and cost of the personnel associated with Physical Plant Operations, whereas in Resource Distribution Services one may wish to determine what percentage of the total staff who possess a MLS degree are concerned with Interlibrary Loan Services. Any level of detail can be developed depending upon the needs of the manager. What is important is the fact that the entire system is constructed so that one is able to put together the answers to questions based on the most detailed levels so as to answer questions at the most general level.

Determining Levels of Activity

By using the NCHEMS Formats and Definitions volume the librarian has readily available the data collection instruments to accomplish the information gathering tasks outlined above. Through the use of several formats, such as the one illustrated in Figure 3, the librarian can picture the human resource and can determine at the same time, through a calculation of percentages, the portion of the total human resource that has been allocated to a category. By examining a second group of data elements, as partially represented by Figure 4, one can determine the allocation of human resources by programmatic activity. By looking at the responsibilities delegated to specialists/librarian personnel within a specific programmatic activity--for example, Machine-Assisted Reference Services (see level three of user services in Figure 2)--the manager can begin to determine what level of activity is generated in light of a specific resource expenditure strategy. This is not to say that the activity is because of this strategy, for there may be slippage, and there are certainly a thousand other variables, but when all of the activity measures are mapped against the total resource allocation pattern

(cont'd. on p. 75)

Figure 3

SERVICE MONTHS BY PERSONNEL CATEGORY

Personnel Categories / Service Months	Service Months of Exempt Employees			Service Months of Nonexempt Employees		
	Executive/ Adminis./ Managerial	Instruct'l/ Research	Specialist/ Librarian	Technical	Office/ Clerical	Service
Service Months of Full-time Employees						
Service Months of Part-time Employees						
Total Service Months						

Figure 4

PERSONNEL AND SERVICE MONTHS BY FUNCTION

Pro-grammatic Activities (Function) / Employee Categories	Headcount					Service Months				
	Exempt Employees		Nonexempt Employees		Total Headcount by function	Exempt Employees		Nonexempt Employees		Total Service Mos. by function
	Full time	Part time	Full time	Part time		Full time	Part time	Full time	Part time	
Administrative Services										
User Services										
Technical/Collection Services										
Instructional Services										
Support Services										
TOTALS BY EMPLOYEE STATUS (Column totals)										

one can begin to answer the question of what activity is achieved given the pattern of expenditure.

This leads to two major questions: "So what?" and "What if?" The first question is tied up with an attempt to evaluate the current allocation. It seems that there might be three levels of "evaluation" that could be attempted. At the least productive level managers, operators, and users could note that "they feel" that good service is provided. While this is not very precise, it does characterize the manner in which many operate or manage, and it is characteristic of portions of many users' surveys.

At the next level libraries that had decided to use the philosophy and the definitions of the data base could compare activity levels. Although the warning noted above about the comparison of activity levels is applicable in this case, this approach still has some validity. For years libraries have evaluated themselves by comparing the descriptions of resources with libraries of a similar type. In the past, if one library had only half the number of books that another similar library possessed, it was usually assumed that the larger library was the better. In public libraries, at least, circulation is often compared, but generally on a per capita basis to make the measure more comparable.

There are some positive uses of activity measures. In essence, they can be used in an attempt to evaluate past internal decisions dealing with resource allocation, or they can be used to predict future demand levels. If, for example, the library made a special purchase of 4,000 new books, which were to arrive all at once, then this purchase activity would predict the existence of an extra load on each element of the book processing system. That load could be anticipated and, within resource constraints, planned for. In a case in which control over demand is outside the library historical activity levels are more useful. If every Friday night the college library has been used by only about 200 people, as compared with 1,000 on most Thursday nights, then this information should be taken into account when establishing staffing patterns. Activity measures are most useful in making decisions which increase efficiency and productivity. If the reference desk is staffed by four librarians and altogether twenty questions are answered per hour, of which only two questions require more than fifteen minutes each, then one might feel that there may be slack time. If, through experimentation in staffing, two people were able to handle the same volume, then the activity level becomes a pointer to areas in which efficiency and productivity can be increased. This is not to say that the quality of the transaction was addressed in this exercise. It may be that the same number of queries were handled but the users had to wait for service. The length of the waiting time which is acceptable should be included in the final decision on staffing.

At the third level of library analysis activity measures could begin to lead to a more powerful indication of performance which could be examined from two seemingly opposite aspects: ratio analysis and analysis of the most efficient surfaces. In both cases several similar libraries would make such comparisons as the number of reference questions answered in relation to the cost. The individual library manager could then compare his or her ratio with the average in order to determine where effort might be concentrated to make the system more productive. While it is often assumed that these average figures are the best indicators, there may be cases in which an analysis of the most efficient libraries may yield more useful information for management. In either case the mapping of activity against resources assigned will be an indicator of points for management interest.

Activity can also be misused with ease. If one public library has a circulation of six books per capita and a second very similar public library has a circulation of two books per capita one can say, assuming that a higher circulation is preferred to a lower one, that the first library appears to be doing something better than the second library when it comes to circulation, but one can not say that it is three times better. In fact no relationship can be drawn between the two except the relative one, and then only if all other activity levels as well as all other constraints are similar. What is required for an end product evaluation of libraries, as opposed to the indications provided through activity levels, is the ability to measure performance in light of specific goals and objectives.

Determining Levels of Performance

Work on library-wide performance measures is still in its infancy but the documents produced by NCHEMS do begin to address this area. In what is admittedly a developmental area, both the Library Statistical Data Base and the Handbook look at nine variables that are "most critical to performance." These include: policy effectiveness; resource acquisition; budgetary control; work environment/staff morale; staff competence; operations effectiveness, including user satisfaction; productivity; and accuracy and timeliness. While the Handbook and the Data Base do identify some potential performance measures, it is recognized that performance can be measured only in light of expressed goals and objectives for a specific library.

As an example of the capability of the Library Statistical Data Base as presently constituted, consider the following series of questions: (1) "Do the library collections support the academic programs," or, what is the relationship between the activity of each academic department within the institution and the intellectual resources which form the library's collections? (2) How many circulations can be attributed to people associated with specific academic departments? and (3) Do people use the collections that have been purchased to support them? That is, do people in specific academic departments concentrate their circulations in materials classed in their areas of interest? This is not to contend that these are the only questions that could be answered. It is, rather, intended to be an example of the ability of the Library Statistical Data Base to begin to look at questions related to library performance.

To address questions one and two examine the two Formats from the NCHEMS work presented as Figure 5 and Figure 6. In Figure 5 the impact of each academic department upon the total institution can be described by determining the number of credit hours produced. In institutions which participate in the Informational Exchange Procedures program of NCHEMS these data should be readily available from the institution's planning or budget office. The information can be presented as credit hours produced or as a percentage of the total credit hours produced, and it can be noted at the level of detail (lower and upper division and graduate or by total only) that is deemed necessary. For a complex institution one might assign weights to upper division or graduate credit so that their activity will count more, or one might add a category to describe faculty research. These semester hour figures or their percentages can then be cross-tabulated with the intellectual resources that apply to that academic department. The allocation of resources by department--that is, for example, determining how many books support history--can be accomplished by using a tool such as the one developed for the Colorado Association of College
(cont'd. on p. 80)

Figure 5

SEMESTER CREDIT HOURS TAUGHT AND COLLECTION CATEGORIES BY ACADEMIC PROGRAMS--
ACADEMIC LIBRARIES

| ACADEMIC PROGRAMS | Semester Credit Hours Taught | NUMBER OF TITLES BY COLLECTION CATEGORIES | | |
| | | Print and Print Facsimile Materials | | Nonprint Materials |
		Books and Bookstock	Periodicals	Other Print and Print Facsimile
DISCIPLINE Lower Division Upper Division Grad. Division					
TOTAL					
DISCIPLINE Lower Division Upper Division Grad. Division					
TOTAL					
DISCIPLINE Lower Division Upper Division Grad. Division					
TOTAL					

Figure 6

USER DISCIPLINE VERSUS COLLECTION SUBJECTS ACADEMIC LIBRARIES

CATEGORIES OF COLLECTION												
USER DISCIPLINE	LC/DEWEY	HEGIS	LC/DEWEY	HEGIS	LC/DEWEY	HEGIS	LC/DEWEY	HEGIS	LC/DEWEY	HEGIS	LC/DEWEY	HEGIS
					Number of General Circulation Transactions							
DISCIPLINE												
Undergraduate												
Graduate												
Instruction/research												
Other employee												
TOTAL												
DISCIPLINE												
Undergraduate												
Graduate												
Instruction/research												
Other employee												
TOTAL												
DISCIPLINE												
Undergraduate												
Graduate												
Instruction/research												
Other employee												
TOTAL												
DISCIPLINE												
Undergraduate												
Graduate												
Instruction/research												
Other employee												
TOTAL												

and University Presidents. This "Crossover Matrix" relates
Library of Congress and/or Dewey Decimal classifications to
the HEGIS codes which are used to describe the academic
departments. An example of this concept, which is shown
in Figure 7, should provide at least an approximate tally of
the number of cataloged library items that should be allocated
to each academic discipline. When the format of Figure 5
is completed one should have at least an approximate answer
to the question of how well the present collection supports the
curriculum.

Figure 7

HEGIS-LIBRARY OF CONGRESS
CROSSOVER MATRIX

(sample section)

HEGIS NUMBER	HEGIS CATEGORY	LC NUMBER
2200	Social Science	HF 1-5000
5000	Business and Commerce Technologies	HF 1-5000
5700	Science or Engineering Related Organized Oc- cupational Curriculum	HF 1-5000
0500	Business or Management	HF 5001-9999
5000	Business and Commerce Technologies	HF 5001-9999
5700	Science or Engineering Related Organized Oc- cupational Curriculum	HF 5001-9999
0500	Business or Management	HG 1-3542
5000	Business and Commerce Technologies	HG 1-3542

The second and third questions, of who uses the collection and do they use those materials that were purchased
to support their activities, can be approached through Figure
6. Here one can take the population of a department and
match it against the circulation activity generated by the types
of materials listed in Figure 5 which have been subdivided by
Library of Congress or Dewey Decimal classification groups.

An analysis of the correlations between the two formats, Figures 5 and 6, should provide information which could begin to evaluate the holdings of the library given the interests of its users. While there are a number of intervening variables, such as the reliance of the discipline on specific forms of materials (e. g. , history on books and chemistry on journals), it seems intuitively pleasing that since total library resources are constrained, there should be some positive correlation between collection strengths and major areas of academic activity. This correlation might be a measure of collection development policy performance.

CONCLUSION

To think that such a system as is presented here would ever be accepted and implemented without extensive analysis, change, manipulation, evaluation, and modification would be naive. It is simplistic to say that one should be able to have external and internal forces coordinated, or to say that all need to come to agreement on the definitions which provide a foundation for the data base. In reality these concepts entail years of intense work by all of the forces that make up American libraries.

The NCHEMS version of this method to analyze libraries has been published but it is not without its rivals. The American National Standards Institute's committee on library statistics is developing a second and different standard. The various national library associations support yet differing versions. Subgroups of those associations are not in agreement. The National Center for Education Statistics is attempting still another set of definitions.

For the individual library manager it becomes difficult to know what the national standard is, or will be, or, indeed, if there ever will be one. Yet it is possible for the individual to do several things. One can look at the difficult environment and recognize the problems of resource constraint. One can look for the interrelationship in the variables within the situation. One can accept the premise that library performance defined in user terms is more meaningful than scattered statistics or simple activity analysis.

On another level the individual librarian can take another step. The need for comparative data, which are gathered in a way that enhances analysis, transcends national library

politics.   The simple fact is that libraries cannot wait much
longer.   It is encouraging to see some uses of such plans as
the NCHEMS work.   The Bibliographic Center for Research,
for example, has used the information presented in Figure 1
as a way of looking at libraries as it developed a long-range
plan for a library network.   Some individual libraries in California have adopted the NCHEMS approach.   For the most
part, however, library statistics analysis is stalled as groups
wrangle over "the" right definition or "the" right approach.
It is the basic contention of this paper that, as librarians
enter the 1980s, the environment will become more, not less,
difficult.   Libraries, if they have a coordinated plan, will be
better able to make do with less.   The importance of a ra-
tional data collection and analysis effort has been presented.
What is needed now is agreement about an accepted method
for data gathering and analysis.   While we may be able to
make do if we begin now, we cannot wait much longer to
begin.

Notes

1.   American Library Annual for 1956-1957.   N. Y. :   Bowker,
     1957, p. 91.   The Bowker Annual of Library and Book
     Trade Information (22d ed.) N. Y. :   Bowker, 1977, p. 35.
2.   Publications produced by NCHEMS as cited in this paper
     are available from the National Center for Higher Educa-
     tion Management Systems, P. O. Drawer P, Boulder,
     CO   80302.
3.   See for example, the College and University Libraries,
     Fall 1979 Survey Part II, Section B, line 16.

THE LIBRARY COURSE FOR CREDIT:
PROBLEMS AND OPPORTUNITIES

by Elizabeth S. Burns

Abstract

Academic librarians are increasingly concerned over the lack of proper training undergraduates are receiving in library research methods. Offering a library course for credit is one way to provide such training. Before undertaking to introduce such a course, librarians must be fully committed to the idea of formal teaching. They must also be prepared to encounter some difficulties in gaining approval for such a course from the college faculty and administration. Considerable determination may be needed to overcome these difficulties. If the library course is successful, new opportunities for teaching research skills to undergraduates may result.

Introduction

> If librarians are truly interested in making sure their students are not only getting educated but staying educated and if they aim to help students become independent researchers and independent library users, then they must try very hard to provide them with systematic and need-oriented library instruction in their regular curriculum. [1]

The library course for credit, taught by librarians, is now part of the curriculum at many institutions of higher learning. It is one of several methods of teaching library skills to undergraduates. A library course for credit, like other academic offerings, meets on a regular basis, within a certain time frame, and has a definite subject content. The differences between the library course for credit and other academic courses lie partly in the library course's greater

emphasis on the techniques of information retrieval, and partly in its use of librarians as teachers.   These differences
may mean that college faculty may not understand either the
necessity for offering such a course, or the desirability of
using librarians to teach it, so that getting a library course
for credit accepted and actually operating may require a determined effort by the librarians.   However, the opportunities
a formal course can provide for training students more effectively in research skills are an important consideration
for those academic librarians who are interested in promoting
this kind of instruction.

As recently as 1972, the Carnegie Commission on
Higher Education reported that libraries were often looked
upon as rather passive centers on campus where books were
kept and where students could study.   This attitude is probably a holdover from earlier times when the academic library
was not heavily patronized and the information explosion had
not yet occurred.   Some academic librarians are still satisfied with this approach, while others are looking for ways to
give more effective training in research methods to larger
numbers of students.   Agreeing with the premise that "...
the function of higher education is not only the transmission
of existing knowledge but most certainly also the imparting
of skills for life-long learning and self-education...,"[2] many
librarians are willing to accept the Carnegie Commission's
recommendation that the library become a more active participant in the educational process and that librarians take a
more aggressive approach to the distribution of information.[3]

Most students entering college have no idea how to
use an academic library.   Accustomed to a small high school
library, often staffed by only one professional librarian, they
may be appalled by the size and scope of the academic library.   Yet a great deal of a student's development both as
an individual and as a scholar depends on the ability to use
library resources.   But who is responsible for seeing that
undergraduates develop this ability?   If the responsibility is
not pin-pointed in some way, many students will get through
four years of college without receiving adequate training in
library use.   Librarians are the obvious people to be involved
in teaching research skills.   They have been trained in the
techniques of information retrieval, and they are thoroughly
familiar with the library in which they work.

Traditional Library Instruction

For a long time, orientation programs and brief sessions of bibliographic instruction were the methods most commonly used to teach students about the academic library.
These techniques are still widely used and have considerable
value.   Orientation programs familiarize new students with
the physical arrangement and the atmosphere of the library.
Normally, students are taken through the building in guided
groups and given a quick tour.   These tours are often carried
out as fast as possible, because another party is shortly to
undergo the same process, so that there is virtually no time
for instruction in the use of the collections.   Many freshmen
take courses in which no library work is required, and it
may be a year or more before they need to use the library's
resources.   By that time, they are likely to have forgotten
anything specific they may have learned about the library during an orientation tour.   The one positive, and important,
impression that remains with most students after such a program is that if they need assistance, they should ask a librarian.   General orientation programs are designed to establish a framework of basic knowledge upon which research
skills can ultimately be built, not to teach those skills.   The
purpose is to acquaint students with the library building and
to introduce them to its service, organization, policies and
procedures. [4]   They should give students some understanding
of the librarian's role as a guide to information sources, and
at the same time give the librarians an opportunity to establish a friendly atmosphere which will encourage students to
ask questions.   But such programs are only a stop-gap measure as far as teaching library skills is concerned.   They apply to one particular situation and cannot provide the more
extensive instruction most students need in search strategy
and technique.

In an attempt to make the general orientation program
more meaningful and to ease the strain on the library staff,
some institutions are experimenting with video or slide-tape
presentations, or are providing self-guided, walking tours of
the library for the individual student.   These may be more
effective than a general orientation program, largely because
students can wait until they feel the need for this information
before using the guides.

The next step is some kind of bibliographic instruction,
which may take several forms.   It may be given by the professor in the classroom, by a librarian in the classroom, by

the professor in the library, by a librarian in the library, or by the professor and the librarian acting as a team in either the classroom or the library. Its efficacy depends to a great extent on the amount of time allotted to it. Too often, it consists of only one class session which, if it takes place in the classroom, may be simply a lecture. If the students are brought to the library, students may be shown where needed material is located and given some basic instruction in how to use it. No more than this can be accomplished in so short a time. The professor will not necessarily accompany the class on this occasion, but may simply designate the general subject area to be covered. The librarian may be asked to show the class all the books and indexes in the library that could be used to write a paper in the field of business. While such reliance upon the librarian's judgment may be flattering, it also leaves the librarian uncertain as to the specific items that should be covered and the depth in which to present them. On the other hand, some professors will be very definite not only about the type of material used but about individual titles to be brought to the students' attention. The librarian may be asked to introduce the class to a certain encyclopedia, a particular dictionary, a few indexes and abstracts, special bibliographies, and other reference books in the designated subject field.

In most cases, this bibliographic instruction is geared to one particular term paper or project. With only one class period at the librarian's disposal, instruction in much depth is not possible. However, the students are at least taught, on a necessarily superficial basis, how to use the card catalog, some reference books and some indexes, and how to make simple citations.

Inadequacy of Traditional Library Instruction

It has become obvious, to those librarians who are genuinely interested in seeing students acquire competence in information retrieval, that traditional methods of library-use instruction are not adequate. The problem is that many students seem unable to transfer what they have learned from bibliographic instruction in one discipline to the demands of another discipline. The student may be able to write a paper on a different aspect of the American Revolution as a result of bibliographic instruction for a previous paper on the subject, but totally incapable of locating sources of information on the fruit fly for a natural sciences project. Although

librarians may point out that certain kinds of reference books
are common to most disciplines, and that these materials can
provide access to almost any topic, students generally are not
able to assimilate this at the time.   Often, so much material
is thrown at them in one short session that they fail to get a
sense of the overall arrangement of information in the various
subject areas.   These brief periods of bibliographic instruction are also too short to teach much about the search strategy each student needs to develop in order to complete assignments efficiently and well, or to lay the foundation for continued effective use of the library.   Some librarians feel
strongly that the present methods of term paper clinics and
bibliographic instruction to answer one specific need do not
provide enough training in library research skills and that
"... the general pattern of the organization of scholarship
should be taught on the undergraduate level. "[5]

Faculty Response to the Problem of Teaching Library Skills

Many faculty members are becoming aware that student
needs for library skills are not being met at the undergraduate level, and are beginning to offer their own courses in research methods, or to incorporate bibliographic instruction
into their regular courses.   This can be very helpful if the
professor knows the library well, and/or consults the library
staff on student assignments.   If not, it can be a traumatic
experience, producing frustration in students, professors and
librarians alike.

> Some library instructional attempts are actually
> disastrous and do harm rather than good, as, for
> example, one of the first attempts at library in-
> struction for educationally disadvantaged students
> at Brooklyn College during the summer of 1970.
> The basic-skills experience which was planned for
> this first group of open admission students, before
> their entrance into regular undergraduate classes,
> was planned to emphasize writing skills; library
> skills were a minor consideration.   The instruction
> in the latter consisted of a library assignment that
> was designed without the assistance of a librarian,
> included such questions as 'What are the differences
> between the Library of Congress and the Dewey
> Classification systems?' and was due before the
> scheduled library tours.   Had the department head
> and the instructors tried to construct an initial

> exposure to the college library calculated to create
> abhorrence of the library, they could not have done
> any better. [6]

While this may be an extreme example, librarians have had
enough experiences of this nature to make them wary of leaving all responsibility for teaching students to do research in
the hands of the faculty.

One aspect of the problem is to prepare students for
graduate work, but there is a more immediate aspect to consider.   Many students have trouble completing homework assignments because of unfamiliarity with research methods.
Some faculty, sensing this, seem to feel that it is the student's responsibility to develop library expertise on his/her
own.   Like the ability to read at the proper level, the ability
to use a library is a skill that students are assumed to have
acquired in elementary or secondary school.   This assumption
is a fallacy.   When reading deficiencies are discovered, they
are likely to be corrected by an instructor in remedial work,
but the responsibility for correcting deficiencies in library
skills is generally not considered important enough to be assigned to any one person or group of people.   Upper division
students, in particular, are assumed to have learned how to
use the college library by osmosis.   If they spend enough
time in the building, knowledge of how to use its facilities is
supposed to be assimilated without further effort on anyone's
part.   Unfamiliarity with the library may be responsible for
this attitude among some of the teaching faculty.   Certain
professors will use a research library, if one exists at or
near the institution, but they are unfamiliar with the library
that serves undergraduates and consequently have little or no
idea what it contains.   Some of these teachers will give a
good grade to upper division students who turn in papers based
only on information culled from articles indexed in the Readers' Guide to Periodical Literature.

Why Librarians Should Get Involved in Teaching

Librarians are very much aware that traditional methods of library instruction have not succeeded in teaching students effective use of library resources.   Observing students
actually at work on assignments, the library staff is in an
excellent position to judge a student's rate of progress in research skills.   As a result of their own training, librarians
understand the process of research, and can determine where

each student stands in that respect.   Librarians are also able
to give the assistance needed at whatever level the student
has reached.   The professor sees the finished product.   The
librarian sees, and often oversees, the whole process, including the time wasted because: 1) the student does not know
where to begin; 2) once a beginning has been made, the student may not know how to proceed from there in a logical
manner; 3) of the panic when one source of information fails
and more material must somehow be located; 4) of the problems with footnotes and bibliography.   As a result, many librarians are feeling the need to participate more actively in
the teaching process, and in a more formal way than the
one-to-one basis at the reference desk, or even than is possible with bibliographic instruction.

Librarians have found that the usual type of bibliographic instruction given in conjunction with regular academic
courses is apt to founder because not enough time is allowed
for it, and because faculty will not necessarily follow through
on planned projects unless they see those projects as truly
valuable.   This kind of faculty attitude helped bring about the
downfall of one of the first well-publicized attempts to teach
library skills to undergraduates, the Monteith College library
experiment, which started in 1961-62.   This was a program
of bibliographic instruction for freshmen built into three major fields of study.   Projects and assignments were worked
out by librarians and faculty together.   The experience turned
out to be frustrating because neither the faculty nor the students considered the library component to be of primary importance. [7]   Teachers tended to feel that course content, and
what the student got out of it, were more important than the
methodology of research. [8]   The overall experiment ultimately
failed because it was based on the idea that independent study
would be emphasized, whereas the faculty eventually decided
to follow more traditional teaching patterns. [9]   Later attempts
by other colleges to provide in-depth bibliographic instruction
have been more successful.   Some institutions, however, have
been trying a different approach by developing the library
course for credit.   This is a solution which gives the librarians more visibility in the educational process and allows
them to make a greater contribution towards filling student
needs.   Not all academic librarians will want to teach a formal course.   Those who do will find a certain philosophical
basis in librarianship which justifies that desire.

Philosophical Basis for the Librarian as Teacher

The library serving undergraduates was originally con-
ceived of as having an inherent teaching function, but no one
was quite sure just what this was, or how to implement it. [10]
Traditionally formal teaching has not been considered one of
the primary responsibilities of the library by anyone except
a few librarians. Because of the lack of definite specifications as to their teaching role, librarians have experimented
with various forms of instruction. Four general patterns
have been identified: 1) "underground" library instruction,
in which the library staff does what it can on its own, with
little or no support from the library administration; 2) a designated library instructor position with its own funding but
with no other staff involvement; 3) broad staff involvement,
but with final responsibility for the program resting with one
unit head; 4) broad staff involvement with librarians as co-
ordinators and subject specialists doing most of the teaching.
In this last situation, the subject specialists may be either
college instructors or librarians. The most effective programs are likely to be those which involve the most people
on the library staff. [11] Patterns of instruction will vary according to local conditions but the library course for credit
is one pattern which has proven useful in many different colleges and universities.

Points to Consider Before Deciding
to Offer a Library Course

There are certain things to consider before going ahead
with a full-fledged credit course instead of the more traditional kind of bibliographic instruction. One of them is time.
Much less time is involved in taking one class period, even
for several courses a semester, than in teaching a course.
There is a vast difference between responsibility for one
period of bibliographic instruction in someone else's course,
and total responsibility for content and preparation of a course
meeting two or three times a week. Many adjustments in
scheduling will have to be made, particularly in those departments of the library which provide the instructors, and ideally the staff should be large enough so that the time spent by
the participating librarians in preparation and actual teaching
does not hamper other essential library services. In most
libraries existing staff can probably handle a single upper-
level course. If the course is planned to be part of the core
curriculum required of all incoming freshmen, additional

personnel undoubtedly will be needed to assist the librarians, whose time spent in classroom teaching must necessarily be limited by their other responsibilities.

The greatest expenditure of time will probably come in the first year, when the course is organized. The number of hours spent planning a syllabus, selecting readings and working out projects for students seems astronomical. After the course has once been taught, preparation time should not be as great, even allowing for updating the material and possibly experimenting with different teaching methods.

All this requires a serious commitment on the part of the library staff, even if only one librarian is actively involved in teaching. In a small college, or if the course is a short one of four to five weeks, or in a university which is trying a single course as an experiment, one librarian may be in charge. This may be dangerous in the long run, for if one person is responsible for the course, and that person leaves, or loses interest, it may not be possible to find a replacement. The course may have to be discontinued. If possible, the responsibility can be shared and the library should allow for a certain amount of turnover in the teaching staff. The University of California (Berkeley) started its library course with six instructors. During the first two years in which the course was offered, the average tenure of teaching librarians was two quarters. [12] Three team-teaching librarians can cooperate well in a semester-length course, which divides easily into three broad, general areas, giving each instructor about four weeks of class work, either concentrated or split up as desired. Shelby State College in Memphis, Tennessee uses ten part-time instructors as well as members of the library staff. [13] Even if only one or two librarians are actually teaching, the entire staff will be involved to the extent that it must be willing to cooperate with whatever scheduling adjustments are needed by the teaching librarians.

There should also be a serious commitment to a library course on the part of the library director. A lukewarm response is not enough; active support from this quarter is vital. The library director should be prepared to get into endless correspondence with officers of the college administration and members of the curriculum committee. The director's word usually carries more weight with the administration than do the representations of librarians, and if it is not utilized, the library course may never come into ex-

istence.   The ongoing success of the program also depends
to a considerable extent on the director's commitment to it
and willingness to allow continuing staff participation despite
problems, such as scheduling complications when the course
is running, that may arise.

      The cost factor must also be considered.   Some in-
structional programs have been started with the aid of a
grant.   The National Endowment for the Humanities and the
Council of Library Resources have combined to offer grants
in the area of library instruction.   Most of these grants are
for fairly large-scale undertakings.   All of them are for a
definite time period, after which any on-going program must
find support from within the institution itself.   Those colleges
which embark on a library course without grant funds should
be prepared to spend some of their own money for it.   Teaching a regular course is outside the job description of most
librarians.   Unlike the teaching faculty, librarians are generally not hired with this type of activity in mind.   Should
they receive extra remuneration for teaching a formal course?
Or for any kind of teaching?   Remuneration for course work
may depend somewhat on whether the institution sees the research methods course as merely another service offered to
students by the library, or whether the course is accepted as
an integral part of the curriculum.   In the former case, the
library will probably be expected to absorb the cost of teaching.   The reward for librarians could then consist of having
this teaching experience become a factor in promotion in the
same way as taking additional courses or acquiring continuing
education units.   When vacancies occur on the library staff,
new people can be hired with the understanding that this kind
of teaching assignment will be part of their regular duties.
At Sangamon State University, in Illinois, teaching librarians
have been freed from administrative duties, which have been
taken over by non-professional department heads familiar with
library work. [14]   Hiring an additional librarian to cover for
those who are teaching is usually not feasible because of the
costs involved.   In any case remuneration is most likely to
be governed by established institutional policy governing added
responsibilities for faculty or other staff.

Procedures for Establishing a Library Course

      After considering all these points, if the librarians
decide that they wish to offer a research methods course,
they must follow the usual channels for the acceptance of new

courses at their particular institution.   Because of the differences between a library course and a regular offering, both
in subject matter and in teaching personnel, and because in
many colleges it is still a struggle to establish even a program of bibliographic instruction, some preliminary ground-
work may be necessary.   In 1969 the University of California
(Santa Barbara) sent a questionnaire to students to find out if
there was a demand for a library course, and the response
was highly favorable.   East Carolina University wrote to
other universities of similar size to ask for recommendations
for setting up a library course.   In some institutions, the
suggestion of such a course has been received enthusiastical-
ly, as was the case at the State University of New York at
Stony Brook.

In most institutions the procedure is basically the
same.   The first step for the librarians is to gain the support of the library administration.   Sometimes the reverse
happens, and the idea originates with an administrator, who
then must persuade the librarians to undertake the project.
In any case, plans should be carefully formulated within the
library before proceeding further.   These plans should then
be discussed at a meeting of a body such as the library advisory committee, if there is one.   The faculty representatives who serve on this committee can be instrumental in
persuading their colleagues that a library course would be
useful.   If the idea is accepted by the library advisory committee, the librarians should then draw up a detailed proposal,
including the rationale for such an offering, and a course
description.   This should be taken back to the library advisory committee for additional suggestions.

After needed changes have been made, the proposal
should be presented in due course for discussion at a regular
meeting of the body empowered to handle matters concerning
the curriculum.   If accepted there, the proposal is likely to
go to an administrative officer for formal approval.   In a
small college, there will probably be only one curriculum
committee; in a university the structure is more complex,
and there may be several channels to consider.   Many colleges and universities now have special procedures for facil-
itating the offering of courses on an experimental basis.   This
might be the proper approach for the first offering of a library course.

At the University of Connecticut,[15] the route chosen
was the Curricula and Courses Committee of the College of

Liberal Arts and Sciences, as it was felt that the proposed
library course would be thought too practical to be accepted
by the University Senate.   From the Curricula and Courses
Committee, the proposal went to the Dean of that college,
and then to the University Provost for final approval.   In the
process, certain matters of concern arose which had to be
satisfactorily resolved.   These dealt with course level, who
the instructor of record should be, and whether additional
people would need to be hired to cover for those giving the
course.

The last item is important to university administrators.
Unless the proposed course has been presented as a core requirement, the administration will probably not be prepared
to hire extra people, either to help teach or to substitute in
the library for those who do teach.   For the first year or
two, the librarians should be able to teach a single upper-
level course by themselves.   Later, if the library course is
so popular that more than one section is needed, extra help
may be essential.   In any case, the college or university administration should know exactly what it will be expected to
provide for a library course, and it is a good idea to keep
requirements to a minimum.

Possible Problem Areas

The curriculum committee is perhaps the most vital
point in the process.   The first difficulties, if any, will be
encountered here.   If possible, one or more of the librarians
should attend the meeting at which the library course proposal
is presented, to answer questions and describe the function
of the course.   The committee members are likely to want
to know: 1) is this course necessary? 2) who will teach it?
3) at what level? 4) for how much credit, if any? 5) should
it be required, or an elective? 6) what would the content be?

Is a library course necessary?   Cannot library skills
be taught by bibliographic instruction or by independent study
programs?   Certainly they can, but course-related bibliographic instruction as practiced in most colleges does not
provide the in-depth instruction in library skills that can be
supplied by a complete course on the subject.   What about
the library component in the library research methods courses
taught by professors?   These courses appear in the college
catalog under the various departments and by various titles,
but they are all teaching the same thing, i.e., how to do

research for term papers, and this makes for considerable duplication. Several faculty members are tied up because each of these offerings must be taught by an instructor from one particular division, and the students taking the course must also be connected with that division. The natural science professor can't instruct the psychology students, or vice versa. As a matter of fact, most professors are not sufficiently conversant with research materials outside their own discipline to do interdepartmental teaching of this kind. The sensible way to avoid this duplication is to amalgamate all these courses into one course, or two if more than one level is desired, using librarians as teachers, since they are trained in the general techniques of information retrieval.

Members of the curriculum committee may suggest independent study programs as an alternative to a research methods course. Independent study can certainly provide the depth lacking in other forms of library-use instruction. It is perhaps the ideal way to learn anything. But it cannot reach enough students at the undergraduate level, and too much of the librarian's time is likely to be taken up with one individual to make this a satisfactory alternative to a full course. Independent study is not an effective approach to helping a group of people with the same basic needs. Library instruction can be individualized in a group. Projects can be assigned that are tailored to the needs and interests of each person in the class. Independent study as such might better be used as an extension to a lower division library course for those students who wish to explore more fully the field of information science.

Faculty status for the librarians and faculty attitudes towards librarians may also become matters of concern. Even if faculty status does exist, the idea of librarians teaching a course may not be acceptable to some faculty who do not think of librarians primarily as teachers. The matter of academic degrees may be a consideration. At present most librarians who would be involved in teaching such a course are likely to have a MLS, or perhaps a subject MA. If the faculty have strong feelings about degree requirements, it may be necessary to give a faculty member the ultimate responsibility for the library course by making him or her the instructor of record. When a library course for credit was first given at the University of Connecticut, the instructor of record was a faculty member in the English Department, whose only connection with the course was to sign the grade reports. A somewhat better solution might be to have a

librarian appointed as a teaching fellow or lecturer within a
division of the college.   This was the final solution at the
University of Connecticut, where the librarian responsible for
the research course was also appointed as a temporary lecturer in the English Department.   If it is a problem to find
a librarian who is acceptable to other faculty as a teaching
colleague, and if the librarians are really committed to teaching, they may have to be willing to make such compromises.

In an institution which has a library school, a course
in library skills might be taught by library school faculty,
rather than by librarians.   At first glance, this might seem
like a good idea, but it may well not work out in practice.
Library school faculty are apt to be fully occupied with their
own students and not to have the time or desire to work with
undergraduates.   Accustomed to graduate level teaching, they
may find it unrewarding, or even difficult, to develop and
teach a more elementary course.   While their credentials
should be acceptable to the teaching faculty, their entrance
into the area of training undergraduates in library skills may
conflict with the librarians' attempt to become a more integral
part of the teaching process.

Ideally, the librarian with faculty status should enjoy
equal standing with teaching faculty when offering a course in
any aspect of information science.   If there is deep faculty
prejudice against the idea of the librarian as teacher, it can
perhaps be finally dispelled only after the course has been
given, and has been proven worthwhile.   In order to get the
library course accepted in the first place, therefore, librarians may have to seek enough support from the faculty at
large to allow the program to be started, even if only on an
experimental or temporary basis and under less than ideal
conditions.

The possibility does exist, of course, that some librarians will not be good teachers; but not all professors are
good teachers.   A librarian who is capable of answering reference questions, supervising independent study, or giving
occasional sessions of bibliographic instruction may not function well in a regular classroom situation.   Unless the librarians have had previous teaching experience which can be evaluated, there is no way to predict absolutely who will be a
good teacher and who will not.   If none of the librarians have
had experience in classroom teaching, their effectiveness in
other forms of instruction can be used as one basis for judg-
ing possible teaching performance.   Attitude is another basis.

Those librarians who can answer questions adequately but are
not really interested in students and try to keep personal contacts with them to a minimum are not likely to be good teachers.   These librarians will probably not want to teach, and
it would be a mistake to force them to do so.   A teaching
librarian should be a person who actively enjoys working with
students and relates well to them, who can present course
material in an interesting way at the student's level, and who
can develop imaginative assignments and projects.   All this
sounds like, and is, the formula for any good teacher.   In
the case of librarians teaching for the first time and having
to prove themselves in the eyes of both faculty and students,
it is particularly important that high quality instruction be
given.   This may be vital to the success of the library course
and to the acceptance of librarians as teachers by their faculty colleagues.   Good preparation for teaching is, therefore,
essential.   Librarians who feel the need for special training
in the techniques of classroom teaching may take education
courses, or attend one or more of the workshops in library
instruction, which are now being given in major cities several
times a year, at which teaching librarians share their expertise.

        The faculty, either as divisional groups or as members
of the curriculum committee, rather than the librarians, are
likely to decide such matters as course level.   In some colleges a library course will be adopted if it deals with the
basics and is offered to first- and second-year students only. [16]
Other colleges will demand an upper-level course for juniors
and seniors.   At the University of Connecticut course level
was dictated to some extent by the decision to seek approval
through the College of Liberal Arts and Sciences, rather than
from the University Senate.   All freshman courses must be
approved by the latter body.   Failure to seek approval there
automatically put the course at a higher level, open to juniors
and seniors and, by permission only, to sophomores.   Sometimes it is a matter of semantics.   At Roger Williams College, Bristol, R. I. , the word "fundamentals" had to be deleted
from the course description before the faculty would consider
it.   The librarians were proposing to offer a research methods course to juniors and seniors who were already supposed
to know the fundamentals.   One professor remarked, "We
are not interested in supporting a course that is going to
teach students how to use the card catalog. "

        In some cases, course level does not apply.   Some
universities offer basic courses which are open to all under-

graduates. [18]   In other cases special programs may exist.
The University of Nevada does not wait until students are at
college level; it offers a four-week Introduction to the Library
course for credit to local high school students in the Early
Student's College Prep program. [19]

The amount of credit given for a library course is
determined partly by course length, course level and content,
and partly by the number of credits those in authority are
willing to assign to a librarian-taught course.   The gamut
runs from none at all for a four- or five-week mini-course
to three credits for a semester-length, research methods
course for juniors and seniors. [20]   The librarians must decide
upon the level at which they feel a library course needs to
be taught, the length of the course, and the material they
wish to cover.   They should also be prepared to suggest the
amount of credit they feel students completing the course de-
serve.   The package is then submitted to the curriculum
committee, which recommends the number of credits it thinks
would be suitable.   This can be a difficult stage in the prepa-
rations for establishing the library course.   Failure to reach
a satisfactory agreement on the amount of credit can terminate the entire proposal.

Should the library course be required, or should it be
an elective?   Course level may be a determining factor.
Many academic librarians would feel that a basic course in
library skills should be required of all entering students,
with the exception of transfer students if they have had such
a course elsewhere.   Shelby State College's course in Library
Use and Information Sources has been part of the core curriculum for the past three years.   East Carolina University
also has a freshman requirement in library skills.   From
the librarian's point of view, this would seem an excellent
goal at which to aim.   It guarantees every student training
in the skills needed for a successful and satisfying college
experience, and for personal enrichment, whether or not the
student continues with formal education or enters an advanced
degree program.   An offering in research methods at a higher
level might well be an elective, primarily for the benefit of
those who plan to attend graduate school.

A question frequently asked by faculty about a proposed
course in library research methods is: what would its content
consist of? It sounds to them like sheer methodology.   But a
strong case can be made for the subject content of a course
in information science.

> Just as mathematics is a discipline in itself, and
> in addition, can be utilized in other disciplines, so
> information science is a discipline in itself, and
> in addition serves to improve the performance of
> students in all other disciplines. Viewed as a dis-
> cipline dealing with communication among people,
> and particularly with the principles and mechanism
> of the transfer of knowledge, information science
> contains a body of knowledge which is indispensable
> to the student and necessary for every educated
> person. [21]

Course content is usually spelled out in the syllabus or outline required at most institutions. Though the arrangement
may vary, it usually includes: introduction to the particular
library being used; access points like the card catalog, bibliographies, abstracts and indexes; reference material, both
general and specialized; periodicals and newspapers; documents; and perhaps microforms. Freshman courses are
usually content to cover the fundamentals only. Upper level
courses may introduce the student to resources important for
future research which the undergraduate library may not hold
in depth, and also of the computerized searching tools now
becoming more widely available. Other topics of interest
may be included, such as the history, function, and organization of libraries, or audio-visual materials. As a corol-
lary to the content, projects should be assigned to help the
student develop a search strategy that will serve no matter
what the subject, and to provide familiarity with the process
of information retrieval.

How is a library course to be evaluated? All regular
courses can be evaluated on the basis of stated goals, content, and teacher performance. The library course is no
exception and should be evaluated in the same way. In course
syllabus or outline, goals should be clearly stated; definite
subject areas should be covered; a certain standard of performance should be expected of the teaching librarians; and
a measurable amount of work to be produced by the students
who should, as a result of taking the course, have acquired
a certain proficiency in the ability to do research should be
defined. Often students are asked to give a written evaluation
of such a course after they have taken it. These evaluations
can be used to determine its future direction and emphasis.
Many research methods courses began on an experimental
basis in answer to a felt need. After the first year or two
of teaching, changes may be advisable, not so much in con-

tent as in format.   Shelby State College started with a traditional lecture course.   By 1976, it was trying to develop a
more individualized approach in order to be more effective.
Cooke County College, Gainesville, Texas, went from the
lecture format to an audio-tutorial cassette program which
combines a 15- to 20-minute taped lecture with a written
workbook assignment. [22]   If the research methods course is
to continue successfully, the librarians need to be flexible
in their approach.

The mechanics of fitting a library course taught by
librarians into the existing framework of the institution can
cause problems.   If the college is divided more or less rig-
idly along departmental or divisional lines, the library course
must somehow be integrated with these.   One or more of the
divisions must be persuaded to include the research methods
course among its other offerings.   If enough departments are
amenable, the library course may be given its own identifying
number which applies in all areas, as, for instance, American Studies 343, Social Science 343, Psychology 343.   This
may look like three different courses in the catalog, but it
is actually only one.   Some universities have interdepartmental courses which are open to students from all disciplines. [23]
The library itself may be considered a separate division for
teaching purposes, and permitted to offer courses. [24]

Unless it is part of the core requirement, some public
relations work may be necessary after the library course is
established.   Librarians must be prepared to advertise an
upper-level course when it is first offered.   Most of this
publicity will be by word of mouth to those students who have
previously expressed an interest in learning more about research methods, and to those students who obviously need
such instruction.   Posters advertising the library course may
be put up on library bulletin boards.   If the library course
is offered in one semester only, a memo can be sent to faculty advisors just before the registration period, reminding
them that the library research course will be given in the
coming term.   If the library course is not publicized enough,
it may fail for lack of students.   Unlike the academic departments, the library has no regular student constituency and
must depend, in the beginning at least, on such advertise-
ment.   All courses ultimately stand or fall on their enrollment.   If the library course turns out to be a good one, and
fills a need, the students themselves will be the best adver-
tisement in ensuing years.

Examples of More Extensive Library Instruction Programs

A library course for credit should not necessarily be considered an end in itself.   Unless it is a core requirement, as at Shelby State College and East Carolina University, it will not reach all those who could profit from it.   It may be necessary to start in a small way, offering only one course in library research methods, but if the course is successful, it may be the entering wedge for a more extensive program of library instruction at a particular institution.   The City University of New York's Bernard Baruch College has developed an entire program consisting of an introductory course and advanced courses on information science in specific disciplines.   Acting as an academic department, this library has established a series of courses which tie in with all the other departments of the college. [25]   The best programs are those which permeate the divisions of the college and reach the most students.   Earlham College in Richmond, Indiana and Sangamon State University in Springfield, Illinois have accomplished this by pooling the efforts of faculty and librarians to incorporate instruction in research methods as widely as possible throughout the institution.

In particular Sangamon State University, which opened in 1970, planned from the beginning to use the training in library skills as an integral part of the teaching process.   The teaching function became the primary responsibility of the professional librarians.   In order to do this, Sangamon State developed a new organizational model which freed the librarians from routine administrative duties by turning these over to non-professional support staff.   The librarians were thus able to spend most of their time in teaching or closely related activities.   They could act as liaison between the faculty and the library, cooperate with professors planning student assignments, and point out how to develop research skills by using course projects.   The librarians also prepared guides to library resources for individual students and arranged reference workshops for groups of students.   The goal of all this was to help students learn research methods and enable undergraduates to attain a higher level of bibliographic sophistication than they are usually able to reach by traditional methods of library instruction. [26]

Conclusion

It should be noted that Sangamon State University opened

as a new institution with the premise that librarians should
serve as teachers in the area of research skills.   While this
may be the ideal solution, it is not always easy to implement
in an older college or university which is already set in a
certain mold of instruction, and has preconceived ideas about
the place of librarians in the academic educational scheme.
A lot of persuasion may be needed to convince the faculty
and administration that librarians do have an inherent teaching function and can contribute in this way to the educational
program of the college.   Once this teaching function is recognized, cooperation between faculty and librarians should improve, even to the extent of using more and better quality
bibliographic instruction in regular college courses in addition
to the library research methods course itself.

        In order to take advantage of the opportunities that may
arise, the teaching librarians must be flexible, and be able
to change their approach to teaching as the situation around
them changes.   There has been a lot of recent publicity about
projected curriculum changes at institutions like the University of California (Berkeley) and Harvard University.   After
the experimentation of the 1960s, when undergraduates at
many colleges could in essence develop their own programs
from a wide assortment of electives, the pendulum is now
beginning to swing back to a more structured curriculum with
more specific requirements. [27]   This may affect upper-level
library research methods courses, because students will have
fewer choices outside the core curriculum.   It does not affect
the basic premise that undergraduates need training in the
science of information retrieval, and it will probably not affect the necessity for librarians to be active in promoting
such training.   Change may mean opportunity.   In any period
of change, librarians have an opportunity to make their concerns known and to speak out for proper undergraduate training in the organization of knowledge and in the techniques
needed to appropriate that knowledge.

        The library course for credit is not a panacea for all
the problems of teaching research skills to undergraduates.
Initially the library course may even present some problems
of its own, of the kind that have been discussed above.   In
some institutions certain of these problem areas are easily
resolved; at other institutions the proposal for a library
course for credit may founder over a single point which cannot be satisfactorily worked out.   If librarians are persistent
and willing to make adjustments to their original plans, they
may still be able to offer a good program of instruction in

research methods, which may ultimately lead to more extensive education in library use.   The goal of all such programs
should be to give undergraduates enough familiarity with information retrieval to enable them not only to have a more
satisfactory experience in college and graduate school, but
also to continue their education for the rest of their lives.

Notes

1. Hannelore B. Rader.   "The Humanizing Function of the
    College Library, " Catholic Library World 47:279-80,
    1978.
2. Ibid. , p. 279.
3. The Carnegie Commission on Higher Education.   Reform
    on Campus: Changing Students, Changing Academic Pro-
    grams.   N. Y. :   McGraw Hill, 1972.
4. Association of Research Libraries.   ARL Management
    Supplement 5:1 (September, 1975).
5. Patricia Senn Breivik.   Open Admissions and the Aca-
    demic Library.   American Library Association, 1977,
    p. 33.
6. Breivik, p. 33.
7. Patricia Knapp.   The Monteith College Library Experi-
    ment.   N. Y. :   Scribners, 1966, p. 153.
8. Ibid. , p. 39-40.
9. Breivik, p. 35.
10. A. B. Passarelli and M. D. Abell.   "Programs of Under-
    graduate Libraries and Problems in Educating Library
    Users, " in J. Lubans, ed. , Educating The Library User.
    N. Y. :   Bowker, 1974, p. 116.
11. A. J. Dyson.   "Organizing the Academic Library for In-
    struction, " Journal of Academic Librarianship 1:11-3,
    1975.
12. Charles Shain.   A Bibliography Course at U. C. Berkeley.
    (Paper submitted to the California Library Association
    Conference in San Francisco, December 11, 1969), p. 3.
13. Unless otherwise noted, all references to colleges and
    universities are from material supplied by The Library
    Orientation Exchange (Project LOEX), Center of Educa-
    tional Resources, Eastern Michigan University Ypsilanti,
    Michigan   48197.
14. H. W. Dillon.   "Organizing the Modern Library for In-
    struction, " Journal of Academic Librarianship 1:4, 1975.
15. All references to the University of Connecticut are from
    material supplied by Norman D. Stevens, University Li-
    brarian.

16. East Carolina University, Nassau Community College, Garden City, N. Y., Central Michigan University, and Arizona State University are among the institutions offering lower division courses.

17. All references to Roger Williams College are based on personal observation.

18. University of California (Berkeley) and the University of the Pacific.

19. LJ/SLJ Hotline (April 25, 1977).

20. The State University of New York's College of Environmental Science and Forestry offers a brief mini-course for no credit; the University of Arkansas at Little Rock and Roger Williams College offer thirteen-week upper-level courses for three credits; while two credits are given for courses at the University of California (San Diego) and Nassau Community College, to name but a few.

21. Thomas Atkins. "Libraries & Academic Instruction," LACUNY Journal 3:14, 1974 (Fall).

22. Weldon J. Horton. "New Dimensions in Innovations; from Problems to Opportunities," Learning Today 8:22-3, 1975 (Summer).

23. The State University of New York at Stony Brook and the University of California (Santa Barbara) offer Interdisciplinary 101. Western Michigan University has General Studies 241, the University of California (San Diego) offers Contemporary Issues 50, and Christopher Newport College of William and Mary has Communications 395.

24. Library 1001 at the University of the Pacific, Library Science 2310 at the University of Arkansas at Little Rock.

25. Atkins, p. 14.

26. Dillon, p. 4-7.

27. Malcolm G. Scully. "Tightening the Curriculum: Enthusiasm, Dissent, and So What Else Is New?" Chronicle of Higher Education (May 8, 1978).

LAW ON-LINE: THE DEVELOPMENT
OF COMPUTERIZED LEGAL SEARCH SERVICES

by Wes Daniels

Abstract

The field of legal research has been the first to see the successful development and implementation of a large-scale natural language, full-text system of interactive on-line retrieval of its source material. With origins in experiments conducted some twenty years ago, two such systems are currently commercially available. Successful implementation of these systems has been feasible because of the structure of legal literature and its linguistic characteristics; the nature of the use and the users of legal material; and the economic base available for legal search services. A trend toward more widespread development of similar systems would have important implications for librarians.

Introduction

Not many years ago, it seemed only visionary to consider the possibility of searching a machine data base using natural language--ordinary words and phrases of the searcher's choice[1]--and retrieving from that data base, visually on a terminal screen or in hard copy, the full text or any or all of several significant portions of a given text.

That possibility is today a reality in the field of legal research. Two major commercial firms have developed such systems, and two agencies of the United States government are using their own versions.

What are the historical antecedents of these developments, and how has it been possible for this remarkable search capability to come into being in law? Does this phenomenon represent the beginning of a trend in machine-based academic research? If so, how should librarians interpret its significance in terms of their traditional role?

The Development of Legal Search Systems

Legal research in the Anglo-American world has been conducted since the decisions of tribunals began to be recorded and accorded precedential value. From the British Plea Rolls of the early twelfth century to the present-day multiplicity of published decisions (over 30,000 court decisions are currently published each year, adding to a collection of over 3,000,000 printed cases)[2], lawyers have sought to bolster their courtroom arguments with citations to prior determinations of legal and factual situations similar to their own. The traditional doctrine of stare decisis ("to abide by decided cases") means that once a court has applied a particular legal concept in a given way, people should be able to rely on the same judicial interpretation in subsequent analogous situations. This has necessitated subject access to the great body of decisional literature, much of which is published chronologically; that is, in the order in which the decisions are rendered, rather than in any conceptual arrangements.

At the same time, the law is in a constant state of flux. In a hierarchical court system, where a higher court can overrule a decision of a lower tribunal, and in a system in which the judiciary can invalidate acts of the legislative and executive branches of government, verification of the continued validity of a past judicial decision, legislative enactment or administrative regulation has also been necessary. Thus lawyers have had first of all to find cases similar to theirs in which the types of decisions which would be favorable to their clients have been reached. They then have had to determine whether those decisions remain valid; that is, whether or not they have been overruled by a higher court.

The information explosion occurred in law long before it did in many other fields. This led, at the end of the nineteenth century, to what has been referred to as "the first revolution in legal research," a revolution consisting of the development of a sophisticated bibliographic apparatus unparalleled in its time.[3]

To deal with the problem of determining the continued validity of a document, a massive set of manual citation indexes called Shepard's Citations began to be devised. By searching a citation in Shepard's a researcher is provided with the citations to subsequent cases which have cited the earlier document, often with some indication of the way in which it was treated in the later text.

For the purpose of finding cases in a certain subject area, a large, multi-form body of legal reference material has accumulated. Among the innovations introduced to enable lawyers to perform this aspect of their research function was the West Publishing Company's key number digest system, which summarizes and assigns subject codes to judicial decisions. The decisions themselves are published chronologically, and the summaries, or headnotes as they are called, are also published in a separate set of volumes, comprising a digest, arranged alphabetically by broad subject categories, with many hierarchically organized subdivisions. General subject and case name indexes provide additional points of access to the main part of the digest.

Another important development was the annotated statutory compilation or code, which rearranges by subject those statutes enacted and initially published chronologically, and which provides references to useful primary and secondary research material, including court decisions interpreting the various legislative enactments.

Further innovations were the introduction of the pocket part and loose-leaf services, which provide for much more frequent revision than had previously been possible.

"The ingenious innovations of the first revolution in legal research," however, "have begun to falter and creak...."[4] There has been a steady increase in reported judicial decisions, and a rise in the importance of statutory (legislative) materials. Recent decades have also witnessed a proliferation of administrative regulations and rulings, emanating from the executive branch of the federal and state governments and from independent regulatory agencies. These administrative documents, which are analogous to statutes and court decisions, have become not only more numerous but also more influential in determining the conduct of individuals and groups, and thus require the increasing attention of a growing number of lawyers.

The result is that the amount of time and effort needed for thorough and comprehensive manual research, especially on complicated legal topics, has become immense. The expense involved increases proportionally, both in financial terms and in terms of the quality of the administration of justice.

Enter the Computer

Computerized approaches to the research problems of
lawyers began to be considered in the 1940s. The earliest
suggestion for an automatic retrieval system came from Louis
O. Kelso in 1946. His article, "Does the Law Need a Technical Revolution?" advocated the development of a "Lawdex"
system in which two technologies then in their infancy would
be applied to legal research. Kelso optimistically predicted
that by combining the micropublication of documents with the
use of "electronic selection" techniques, it would be possible
to perform "instantaneous" and "absolutely exhaustive" searches
which would retrieve "all relevant data. "[5]

The first actual machine application was developed about
a decade later to meet a concrete research need. In order
to prepare a manual on hospital law, John F. Horty and his
colleagues at the University of Pittsburgh Health Law Center
were required to search manually the statutes of all fifty
states for relevant material. Having spent over two years
on the task, they concluded that there had to be an easier
way, and they began exploring the possibility of computer
applications.

Horty had been faced with the lack of a single set of
printed indexes for all American statutory law, a lack of uniformity in the indexes for the various states, and the failure
of the indexes to keep pace with new terminology in expanding
or emerging subject areas. Accordingly, one of his goals
was to design a system which would allow for full-text searching, thus obviating completely the need for indexing. Likewise, rather than submit to the restrictions of a closed vocabulary list of searchable terms, he planned to allow for
the use of natural language in formulating search requests.

By having all of the Pennsylvania statutes key-punched
into machine-readable form, Horty successfully demonstrated
an off-line system for storage and retrieval of statutes at
the 1960 American Bar Association convention. The system
used a "Key Word in Combination, " natural language approach,
which allowed the searching of any word or phrase in combination with any number of other words or phrases. The data
base was expanded to the extent that Aspen Systems Corporation, founded by Horty, could in 1970 offer the full texts of
the statutes of all fifty states and the federal statutory compilation, the U.S. Code. This company continues to provide
off-line legal research services today.

Horty's system was organized on the concordance principle. Each word in every document (excluding a number of very common, non-substantive words, such as articles) was listed in the computer, with each location of that word in the data base. Initially, only the number of the document containing the word was indicated. As early as 1962, however, the concordance was refined to provide the exact location of each word within each document. The use of a proximity connector was also available, so that the appearance of a combination of terms within the same sentence could be specified.

This work led to the development by the U. S. Air Force, in the early 1960s, of LITE (Legal Information Thru Electronics), an off-line system containing statutory and regulatory material and some case law, primarily in the accounting and finance areas. Now called FLITE (adding "Federal" to the title), it is still being used, almost exclusively by the Defense Department.

The early efforts at full-text, natural language retrieval of legal documents focused on statutes. The West digest system, which arranges summaries of court decisions by subject, already provided some help to the researcher of comparative case law, but no such master indexes existed for legislation. Also, there was a feeling that "statutes are carefully framed in words chosen for clarity rather than literary quality,"[6] whereas "judges want their opinions to read like literary works of art"[7] and will therefore attempt to vary phraseology. It was foreseen, then, that word searching, as opposed to subject searching, would be more productive in a statutory data base than in one containing court decisions.

It is somewhat ironic, therefore, that LEXIS and Westlaw, the two commercial on-line, interactive, full-text, natural language legal search services which exist today, contain a much larger body of judicial decisions than anything else. Perhaps the major reason for this development is the expense involved in updating statutory material to reflect changes made in each legislative session.

LEXIS had its origins in a study conducted by the Ohio Bar Association in the mid-1960s. Concluding that no satisfactory computer search system then existed in law, the Association decided to develop its own. It established a nonprofit subsidiary, Ohio Bar Automated Research (OBAR), and in 1967 entered into a contract with the Data Corporation, which later became Mead Data Central (MDC), a subsidiary of Mead Corporation. What had recommended the Data Corporation was its development several years earlier of a system for the retrieval of Air Force reconnaissance documents.

During 1969, fifteen teletype terminals (changed to cathode ray tubes, CRTs, a year later) were set up experimentally in lawyers' offices in Ohio, and MDC studied the performance of the system it had designed. Concluding that it was both effective and economically feasible, OBAR slated the project for full production within the state.

The data base consisted of primary Ohio legal materials: the state's Constitution, statutory code, and appellate court decisions. The system used full-text and natural language, which it had in common with the Horty approach. Innovations, however, were introduced. It accessed the full text randomly, as opposed to the more time-consuming sequential searching of other systems; and it was interactive, on-line, so that a researcher could obtain immediate feedback on the relative success of his/her search strategy, and modify that strategy accordingly.

Meanwhile, the West Publishing Company, the largest legal publisher in the world, was becoming involved in similar efforts. It sued Law Research Services, probably the first commercial firm to launch a legal retrieval service (in 1964), for allegedly using an indexing system copied from West's key number scheme.

West's own computerized legal search system, Westlaw, was initiated in 1976. It is an adaptation of the Canadian QUIC/LAW system (Queen's University Institute for Computing and Law), developed in the early 1970s by a combined research effort of Ontario's Queen's University and IBM Canada. [8]

JURIS (Justice Retrieval and Inquiry System), which became operational in 1972, was developed by the U.S. Department of Justice as an on-line retrieval system using West key numbers to index a data base comprised of material generated within the Justice Department, as well as federal cases in full text and the headnotes, or summaries, of state cases. This system is in use today throughout Justice Department and United States Attorneys' offices across the country, but is not available to the public.

Today's Commercial Systems

LEXIS and Westlaw, the two major commercial competitors for the automated legal research market today, are
available to a variety of law libraries.   Beginning from somewhat different premises, the two systems have become increasingly similar.

From its initial file of Ohio material, LEXIS expanded
to provide selected "libraries," or data bases, containing the
the full text of court decisions, constitutions and statutes from
the federal level and selected states, and some federal administrative regulations and rulings in the fields of income
taxation and securities regulation.   Mead has continued to
add the court decisions of additional states, as markets for
those materials developed.   These files have been available
retrospectively to various dates, depending on the file.   By
the end of 1979, the reports of cases from all fifty states
and the District of Columbia finally had been made available,
at least back to January 1978.   Statutes are currently available only on the federal level and for four states (Ohio, New
York, Kansas and Missouri), and Mead has not indicated any
intention to expand this category.

By using any word and/or phrase of his/her choosing,
the searcher can access the LEXIS "libraries" to retrieve
material relevant to a legal problem.   These words and
phrases can be combined by the Boolean algebra techniques
common to many other search systems, that is by using the
connectors AND, OR, AND NOT, BUT NOT, etc. [9]   Proximity connector keys can be employed to retrieve texts in which
one word or phrase being searched occurs within a given
number of words of another search term.   Thus, the searcher may request all decisions in which the word "physician"
or "doctor" or "surgeon" occurs within five words (or any
number up to 255) of "negligence" or "malpractice."   That
portion of each case containing that combination may be dis-
placed on the CRT screen, and any or all of the complete
decisions (or, more commonly, only the citations to those
decisions, because of the expense involved) may be printed
on-line on an attached hard-copy printer.   Law firm LEXIS
users, but not law library users, have the option of having
material printed off-line and mailed.

Searches may also be restricted to certain segments of
documents, such as the name of the case, date of decision,
majority or dissenting opinion, or the name of the judge

writing an opinion.   This feature makes it possible to retrieve
quickly and efficiently certain types of information not available in any way through manual search techniques.   It is possible, for example, to identify all opinions on a certain subject written by a particular judge.   Further, the searcher
may specify that a combination of search terms must appear
in the same segment in order to satisfy the request.

   In addition to words or phrases, numbers or combinations of numbers and words can be searched.   It is therefore
possible to retrieve cases which have cited a previous case
or statute, by entering its alphanumeric citation (e. g. , 367
U. S. 643 or 28 U. S. C. 1983) to determine that earlier document's continued validity and/or to find additional material of
potential research value.

   Westlaw, the West Publishing Company's system, is
similar in some respects and different in others.   As mentioned earlier, however, the differences are being reduced.
At its inception in 1976, it provided access only to the headnotes (one-sentence summaries of important points of law
discussed in the case) of court decisions reported in its National Reporter System. [10]   Beginning in 1978, however, it
began to provide access to the full text of these opinions,
largely on a current, non-retrospective basis.

   Westlaw is still somewhat more restrictive than LEXIS
in the types of material it offers, providing only the U. S.
Code in addition to court decisions.   Westlaw had been more
comprehensive in the scope of the decisions its data base
contains, making available cases from the federal courts and
all fifty states.   As noted above, however, LEXIS was able
to offer all fifty states by the end of 1979, and LEXIS' emphasis is increasingly focused on decisions as opposed to
statutes.

   One major difference of the Westlaw system is that it
provides for searching by pre-selected subject terms, based
on its key-number indexing system, in addition to natural
language access.   Another is that it permits the phrasing of
search queries in the form of a question ("May an attorney
in possession of records belonging to a client assert the client's privilege against self-incrimination?"), as an alternative
to the linking of discrete terms ("attorney & client & privilege & incrimination").   In the complete question format, the
system will search each word as if connected by the operator
"OR", and rank the documents retrieved in order according

to the frequency with which the terms searched appear in each decision. By contrast, LEXIS displays documents hierarchically, according to the level of court, and within each court level in reverse chronological order, with the most recent displayed first, regardless of frequency of occurrence of the search terms.

LEXIS and Westlaw, then, began with different philosophical approaches to computer searching in two major respects. Westlaw was based on the view that indexing and abstracting are essential to legal research. This is not surprising, considering the fact that West's business had been built around a system of reporting court decisions using key numbers and headnotes, and by constructing indexes from these features. By initially constructing a data base consisting only of its case headnotes, West was providing a system based on a principle similar to its manual approach.

In searching Westlaw by key number, the searcher essentially uses a controlled vocabulary thesaurus of searchable terms. Even using natural language terminology to search headnotes is a form of subject searching, as the words in the headnote have been selected for their value as indexing terms describing the subject content of the court decision.

One of the principles upon which LEXIS has always been based is the preferability of word searches over subject searches. Natural language searching of full texts is seen as avoiding the limitations imposed by an indexer's subjective pre-determination of relevancy, by the inconsistency inherent in the use of a multiplicity of indexers, and by the impossibility of a controlled vocabulary adequately keeping up with current terminology. West's decision to begin to offer full-text retrieval seems to indicate an admission of the superiority of that approach.

That West may have had to operate at a significant competitive disadvantage had it not begun to offer full-text is suggested by a 1977 report issued by the Federal Judicial Center. Based on the results of a comparative pilot project in which LEXIS and Westlaw were tested in a number of federal court offices, the Center strongly recommended LEXIS, having concluded that "the full-text system outperforms the headnote system by almost every measure."[11]

The other major difference in philosophical premise is illustrated by West's choice of the ranking algorithms approach,

which is based on the assumption that relevance is indicated
by the number of word matches between a query and a document. Thus, in ranking documents according to the frequency
of occurrence of the search terms entered, there is less emphasis than exists in LEXIS on the use of Boolean and proximity connectors. In other words, Westlaw's approach theo-
rizes that relevant documents are more often those which use
the search words most frequently, rather than those which
use them in certain combinations or in close physical proximity.

Characteristics of Legal Literature

Successful implementation of the types of search systems
described above has been feasible in the field of legal research
for a number of reasons, some of which have to do with bibliographic and linguistic considerations.

Legal literature consists of certain categories not usually found in other subject areas. There is a clearly defined
body of primary material which every American legal researcher must use, regardless of his/her personal or professional opinion of the validity or wisdom of the concepts
expressed in those sources. These materials include federal
and state constitutions and statutes, court decisions, and in
some instances administrative regulations and rulings, which
parallel statutes and decisions.

Although lawyers may propose differing interpretations
of statutes or court decisions, they have no choice but to refer to those materials controlling the subject matter of their
cases. They must determine whether or not a legislature
has passed a law or a court has issued an opinion concerning
their legal problem. They may then argue that their case
has distinguishing characteristics, that a statute is unconsti-
tutional (for which argument they must have recourse to the
text of the constitution and to court cases interpreting it),
or they may even argue that a particular court decision was
wrongly reasoned. But there is no avoiding finding the law
or case and considering it as controlling until it is invalidated
by the official act of a court or legislature.

Even legal researchers doing scholarly work, as opposed
to litigation or counseling, must have recourse to these same
primary materials. Legal historians need to find out what
the state of the law on a topic was at a given time. Advocates

of change must refer to those concepts, as embodied in statutes or decisions, which they feel should be reconsidered.

Certain works may be considered classics in fields like
history or literature or sociology, and enjoy wide acceptance
as basic texts for research purposes. There is no comparison, however, with law in the scope or amount of works considered primary, the degree of acceptance of materials as
definitive, or the extent to which large numbers of researchers build upon the very same texts in the development of
their arguments. "No other science ... assigns a place in
the spectrum of the literature apart from all other considerations and solely on the basis of the provenance of the document."[12]

The Language of the Law

Legal vocabulary and its use also differ markedly from
the ways in which language is used in other subject fields.
As linguist Paul L. Garvin has noted, legal dialect has "certain built-in elements of codification," and while to a lawyer
this language may contain a bothersome amount of ambiguity,
there is much less than in ordinary speech, or even than in
scientific speech. Lawyers are "able to make certain distinctions with a rather high degree of unequivocality, compared
to the general degree of unequivocality that you find in ordinary language."[13]

The jargon in many disciplines changes frequently and
a term may have different meanings at different points in
time. Further, the terminology is often not clearly defined
to begin with, and a multiplicity of ambiguous synonyms is
prevalent. Legal language, on the other hand, changes in-
frequently, and terms retain their meaning over time. The
terminology is clearly defined, and the occurrence of synonyms is much less frequent.

Consider the following examples. "Performance con-
tracting in education" (sometimes also called "accountability,"
or other things) is a term which came into existence a few
years ago, and seems to have fallen into relative disuse.
"Free schools" meant something entirely different in 1820
from what the term meant in 1970. The term "assault" in
the law, however, was being used centuries ago to describe
essentially the same concept that it does today. "Poverty"
means many different things to many different sociologists,

and few psychiatrists can agree on a definition of "schizo-
phrenia. " The terms "incompetence" or "vagrancy" have
specialized meanings in law, which all lawyers know and use
in basically the same ways. In common parlance the words
"larceny, " "theft, " "robbery" and "burglary" are often used
interchangeably; in the law, these terms have very precise
and different meanings.

A search system then, based on natural language access,
is much more feasible in legal research than it probably would
be in most other fields. The greater the degree of ambiguity
and synonymity, the greater the need for a controlled, thesaurus-
based vocabulary to assure the retrieval of all related, relevant material through a given search.

The Users of Legal Literature

The field of law is unique in that the great majority of
people doing legal research are practitioners rather than aca-
demics. In the humanities and social sciences generally,
most researchers write and teach; they do not practice literature or sociology, at least in the way most lawyers practice
law. Even in the sciences, where there are many "practicing" chemists, physicians or physicists, there is usually a
distinction between practitioners and researchers. The former put to practical use the discoveries of the latter, but
they do not do the discovering themselves. Most of the people needing access to legal source materials are not university professors, but practicing lawyers. This is significant
in terms of the feasibility of implementing the type of machine-
based search service being discussed here.

Legal practitioners, unlike purely academic researchers,
can pass the cost of their research to the consumer quite directly. The primary customers of LEXIS and Westlaw are
large law firms. Where these systems exist in academic institutions, they are provided at a greatly reduced cost, by
companies which expect that students trained in computerized
legal research will make use of those systems in their law
practice. The law firms can afford these otherwise expensive systems by building their cost into the fee structures
used to charge clients for their services. It may, in fact,
ultimately be no more expensive to conduct research in such
a setting by using a computerized system than by relying on
traditional manual search approaches alone. Even when clients are charged more per hour, the number of total hours

required can be significantly reduced.   If many hours of a
lawyer's research time can be saved through the use of a
comprehensive, quick-response search capability, the system
is capable of at least paying for itself.

And if what meager evidence is available is any indication, the comprehensiveness and quality of that research can
be enhanced.   Even if surveys conducted by the commercial
vendors themselves are discounted for lack of objectivity, the
independent study undertaken by the Federal Judicial Center
concluded that computer-assisted legal research systems save
important amounts of time in some situations, while also improving research quality in finding cases which might not have
been discovered manually. [14]

By contrast, historians and English professors do not
have a commercial financial structure within which to operate.
Even if a faculty member can perform research faster and
easier and more comprehensively using a computer system,
this is not saving anyone any money.   Thus, though faculty
members are often supported by research grants, academia
cannot provide the overall financial base necessary to implement extensive and expensive search services like LEXIS or
Westlaw.

All primary legal source material is in the public domain, and thus exempt from copyright restrictions or fees.
This is an additional advantage that those seeking to provide
computerized search services in law have over people working in other subject areas.

Conclusion

Are the prospects indeed gloomy for the extension to
other subject areas of the types of computer search systems
which have been developed in law?

F. W. Lancaster has recently predicted that "it seems
very likely that we will see increased emphasis on the use of
natural language in information retrieval in the future. "[15]
He mentions a number of efforts being undertaken in scientific
information dissemination centers, the defense and intelligence
communities and elsewhere to implement natural language
search systems.

As the initial generation of texts in machine-readable

form continues to become more widespread, the opportunities for full-text machine retrievability will increase.   The fact that West Publishing Company prints its book-form legal materials by a computer-assisted process certainly increases the financial viability of its computer search system.

There seems, in fact, to be a great degree of compatibility inherent in these two developments.   In economic terms, the increased cost of full-text input is offset by the savings realized by forgoing indexing.

The probable effect of these developments on the role of the librarian remains unclear.   Lancaster notes that controlled-vocabulary systems favor the information specialist, whereas natural language searching, based on the language of practitioners as reflected in the texts they generate, favors the subject specialist.   To the extent that reference librarians lack specific subject expertise, then, their role as intermediaries would be jeopardized if a trend toward natural language systems appears.

Even in the context of controlled-vocabulary searches, the efficacy of this role has been called into question by Lancaster's own research.   In an evaluation of MEDLARS, he attributes a significant percentage of recall and precision failures to the distortion of users' initial requests by librarians overly influenced by the logical and linguistic constraints of the system. [16]

There is some evidence to indicate that, in the context of law firm libraries, the vast majority of LEXIS searches are being conducted by attorneys without the intervention of librarians, [17] very few of whom are also lawyers.

Clearly this means that if librarians expect to exercise much more than a merely custodial function with respect to these systems, they will need to develop specific expertise in the subjects in which computer-assisted research is being done.

Selected Bibliography

Appenzellar, Terry and Robert M. Landau.   "On-Line Information Retrieval for the Legal Profession: A User's Perspective, " Law Library Journal 70:532-49, 1977.

Beard, Joseph J. "Information Systems Application in Law," Annual Review of Information Science and Technology 6:369-96, 1971.

Bing, Jon and Trygve Harvold. Legal Decisions and Information Systems. Oslo: Universitetsforlaget, 1977.

Canada. Dept. of Justice. "Operation Compulex: Information Needs of the Practicing Lawyer," Rutgers Journal of Computers and the Law 2:188-241, 1972.

Chandler, James P. "Computers and Case Law," Rutgers Journal of Computers and the Law 3:202-218, 1974.

Cohen, Morris L. "Computerizing Legal Research," Jurimetrics 14:3-9, 1973.

Computers and the Law Conference, 1968: Proceedings. Kingston, Ont.: Faculty of Law, Queen's University, 1968.

Fiordalisi, Vincent, H. Peter Luhn and Allen Kent. "Progress and Problems in Application of Electronic Data Processing Systems to Legal Research," MULL: Modern Uses of Logic in Law 1960:174-88.

Halladay, Henry. "Legal Research with Westlaw," American Bar Association Journal 61:1414-6, 1975.

Harrington, William G. "Computers and Legal Research," American Bar Association Journal 56:1145-8, 1970.

Harrington, William G. "What's Happening in Computer-Assisted Legal Research?" American Bar Association Journal 60:924-8, 1974.

Horty, John F. "Experience with the Application of Electronic Data Processing Systems in General Law," MULL: Modern Uses of Logic in Law 1960:158-68.

Horty, John F. "Keywords in Combination Approach to Computer Research in Law with Comments on Costs," MULL: Modern Uses of Logic in Law 1962:54-64.

Horty, John F. "Research Report: University of Pittsburgh Health Law Center," MULL: Modern Uses of Logic in Law 1959:31.

Lancaster, F. W. "Vocabulary Control in Information Retrieval System," Advances in Librarianship 7:1-40, 1977.

"The Language of the Machine and the Language of the Law," Law and Electronics: The Challenge of a New Era. Proceedings of the 1st National Law and Electronics Conference, Lake Arrowhead, California, 1960. Albany: M. Bender, 1962.

Meyers, Mindy J. "The Impact of LEXIS on the Law Firm Library: A Survey," Law Library Journal 71:158-69, 1978. .

Meyers, J. M. "Computers and the Searching of Law Texts in England and North America: A Review of the State of the Art," Journal of Documentation 29:212-28, 1973.

National Conference on Automated Law Research, 2d, Monterey, California, 1973. Sense and Systems in Automated Law Research. Chicago: Section of Science and Technology, American Bar Association, 1975.

Sager, Alan M. An Evaluation of Computer Assisted Legal Research Systems for Federal Court Applications. Washington: Federal Judicial Center, 1977.

SEARCH Group, Inc. Automated Legal Research: A Study for Criminal Justice Agencies. (Technical report no. 19) Sacramento, 1978.

Smith, Frederick E. "Some Characteristics of Legal Information and Their Importance in the Economics of Networks," Law Library Journal 70:60-6, 1977.

Sprowl, James A. "Computer-Assisted Legal Research-- An Analysis of Full-Text Document Retrieval Systems, Particularly the LEXIS System," American Bar Foundation Research Journal 1976:175-226.

Sprowl, James A. "Computer-Assisted Legal Research: Westlaw and LEXIS," American Bar Association Journal 62: 320-3, 1976.

Sprowl, James A. A Manual for Computer-Assisted Legal Research. Chicago: American Bar Foundation, 1976.

Sprowl, James A.   "The Westlaw System--A Different Approach to Computer-Assisted Legal Research, " Jurimetrics 16:142-8, 1976.

Troy, F. J.   "Ohio Bar Automated Research--A Practical System of Computerized Legal Research, "   Jurimetrics 10:62-9, 1969.

Notes

1.   The phrase "natural language" in the context of data-base searching is sometimes used in a more restricted sense, to indicate a query formulated just as a question would be posed in ordinary speech, in complete sentence form.   As used generally in the text here, "natural language" searching means the use of any discrete words or phrases the searcher chooses, as opposed to "controlled vocabulary" searching, which restricts the use of search keys to a pre-selected list of terms which the system will exclusively accept.

2.   Cohen, Morris L.   Legal Research in a Nutshell.   3d ed. St. Paul: West, 1978, p. 64-5.

3.   Cohen, Morris L.   "Computerizing Legal Research, " Jurimetrics 14:4, 1973.

4.   Ibid.

5.   Rocky Mountain Law Review 18:378-92, 1946.

6.   Horty, John F.   "Keywords in Combination Approach to Computer Research in Law with Comments on Costs, " MULL: Modern Uses of Logic in Law 1962:56.

7.   Troy, F. J.   "Ohio Bar Automated Research--A Practical System of Computerized Legal Research, " Jurimetrics 10:65, 1969.

8.   Another Canadian legal search system of the early 1970s was DATUM (Documentation Automatique des Textes Juridiques de l'Université), a bilingual, full-text case retrieval system.

9. George Boole, the inventor of Boolean logic, would not have been surprised to see his technique applied to legal research. He used a problem in Jewish dietary law as an example in his work An Investigation of the Laws of Thought (1854). See Jon Bing and Trygve Harvold, Legal Decisions and Information Systems. Oslo: Universitetsforlaget, 1977, p. 59.

10. The basic structure of West's National Reporter System is as follows: decisions of the federal courts are published in four separate series, and the decisions of the state appellate courts in seven regional series.

11. Sager, Alan M. An Evaluation of Computer Assisted Legal Research Systems for Federal Court Applications. Washington: Federal Judicial Center, 1977, p. 121.

12. Smith, Frederick E. "Some Characteristics of Legal Information and Their Importance in the Economics of Networks, " Law Library Journal 70:63, 1977.

13. "The Language of the Machine and the Language of the Law, " in Law and Electronics: The Challenge of a New Era: Proceedings of the 1st National Law and Electronics Conference, Lake Arrowhead, California, 1960. Albany: M. Bender, 1962, p. 120-1.

14. See note 11. Compare, however, the conclusions of SEARCH Group, Inc., a consortium of law enforcement agencies, which held that the automated legal research performed in a study funded by the Law Enforcement Assistance Administration (LEAA) "did not constitute a clear improvement over manual research. " Automated Legal Research: A Study for Criminal Justice Agencies. Sacramento: SEARCH Group, Inc., 1978 (Technical report no. 19), p. 13.

15. "Vocabulary Control in Information Retrieval, " Advances in Librarianship 7:25, 1977.

16. Evaluation of the MEDLARS Demand Search Service. Washington: U. S. Public Health Service, 1968, reported in Stevens, Norman D., "MEDLARS: A Summary Review and Evaluation of Three Reports, " Library Resources and Technical Services 14:109-12, 1970.

17. These data, obtained from a very small sample, were reported in Meyers, Mindy J., "The Impact of LEXIS on the Law Firm Library: A Survey," Law Library Journal 71:158-69, 1978.

FINDING AND UTILIZING NEW INFORMATION RESOURCES IN THE ACADEMIC INSTITUTION

by Kathleen Gunning

Abstract

In most academic institutions there are collections of information resources separate from the main library system. The library staff needs to become more aware of these resources in order to guide users to the full range of available materials. Information about the number and scope of such collections can be obtained by means of a questionnaire. The library staff can then compile a directory of those resources and determine whether or not to establish closer links to them. Such links might include: allowing broader access; obtaining a list of significant items in the collection; adding the records of items in the collection to the library's catalogs; or merging the collection with the library's holdings. Such a project can increase the staff's awareness of those materials, increase access to them, and give the library an opportunity to examine its present collection and service policies.

Introduction

The main library system is not the only collection of information resources maintained by most academic institutions. In addition to specialized information units (e. g., audio-visual centers), there are usually groups of materials of various kinds and sizes which have been assembled by administrative and academic departments, research staff, and special interest groups to meet their needs. Members of the library staff are often unaware of all of these collections. This prevents the effective coordination of the library's collections with those materials, in terms of both current availability and future acquisitions.

Traditionally, the existence of these separate collections has not been considered important by most librarians.
That situation, however, has already begun to change. Two
factors which affect academic libraries are increasing the
probability that library staffs will want to know and need to
know more about such collections.

The first factor, inflation, has reduced the purchasing
power of institutional and library acquisitions budgets and has
prompted many libraries to begin, or at least seriously to
consider, resource sharing with other libraries. It seems
reasonable to expect that economic considerations will also
lead to the coordination and sharing of resources within academic institutions. Certainly colleges and university administrators are likely to be increasingly interested in the cost
savings that may be possible through better coordination of
resources on their own campus.

The second factor is the concept of the library as an
information clearinghouse, which seems to be gaining increasing acceptance. More and more librarians believe that the
public service staff should not only be able to help the patron
use the library's own holdings but should be able to link the
patron to a network of other resources to be consulted when
the materials within the library are inadequate. A central
pool of information within the library about resources available elsewhere can increase the speed and minimize the costs
of obtaining access to them. Certainly any such information
and referral service should include information about the organization and location of other resources and services within
the same institution.

Locating Resources

Should the library staff of an institution decide to find
out what other collections of information exist within the institution, several issues must first be considered. The librarians must choose a method of gathering the information
about those collections as easily as possible. The library
staff then needs to consider ways in which that information
can best be made available, as well as what information the
managers and users of those collections can give the library
about the adequacy of its own collections and services.

In small institutions, where only a few collections are

likely to exist, it might be feasible to telephone the various
offices on campus to gather the information about those resources. For larger schools, and perhaps for some smaller
schools as well, it is probably more efficient to design a
multiple-choice questionnaire to be mailed, with an appropriate
covering letter, either to all departments or, at least, to
those departments or units known, or thought, to have information collections. The letter should clearly explain the library system wishes to identify collections of information resources and to consider ways in which the library might work
more closely with some or all of the units identified to improve the overall availability of access to information for all
faculty and students.

   The library needs to know, of course, not just whether
or not each unit maintains a collection of materials but some
basic information about the nature and content of those collections. Thus the questionnaire should seek to obtain as
much information as possible. It should ask:

   + what types of material are in the collection
   + the size of the collection
   + the present space occupied by the collection
   + the location of the collection
   + whether a catalog of the collection exists or not
   + the way in which the collection is serviced
   + the main source of material
   + the kinds and formats of material
   + who has access to the collection
   + what hours the collection is available for general use
   + whether the collection is unique or duplicates mate-
       rial in the library's collections
   + to what extent the unit's teaching and research de-
       pend upon the resources of the main library system
   + to what extent the main library system owns or can
       obtain items that the members of the unit need
   + whether or not the unit is located conveniently to a
       main library building with collections in its dis-
       cipline.

   Some of the information, such as that pertaining to
duplication with the main library collections, is likely to be
highly impressionistic. Depending upon the nature of the rest
of the information about such an outside collection and the
importance of that collection, the library staff may choose
either to accept the estimate and impression of the respondent
or to verify it through some examination and sampling of the
holdings.

If the library staff has designed the questionnaire carefully to elicit all of the necessary information, the need to
make a number of follow-up telephone calls or inquiries can
be avoided.   Since, as is well known, the response rate to
any questionnaire may be low, the questionnaire should be
as concise and as easy to answer as possible.   In many academic institutions there are faculty members with professional
expertise in the design of questionnaires and it may be useful
to seek their assistance.   Even with a good questionnaire design, however, the staff conducting a survey should be prepared for the necessity of sending out a second round of
questionnaires, and for the possibility of having to gather information from nonrespondents in person or by telephone.   In
this particular process completeness is essential and every
effort should be made to obtain all pertinent information.

The library may undertake such a survey simply to
uncover additional resources for its patrons.   It can also use
such a survey to study the reasons for the creation and per-
sistence of such collections.   Genaway and Stanford have published a study of the common characteristics and causes of
"quasi-departmental" libraries at the University of Minnesota
in relationship to the services provided by the central library
system. [1]   They found that such collections can exist to provide duplicates of library materials at closer proximity or
with greater reliability than in the central system.

If these materials are not owned by the library, then
some consideration of why that is so should be undertaken.
They may be outside the scope of the library's collections because of their form or subject matter.   If they are within
that scope, the library may wish to investigate why they were
not selected for purchase.   The library might be able to use
this information as a basis for reexamining its collection and
service policies, and making such adjustments in those policies as might be desirable.

As the questionnaire responses are submitted, the library staff can evaluate the information to determine possible
levels of cooperation between the library system and the independent collections.   Then the library staff can set goals
as to the levels of cooperation to be achieved.   This goal-
setting must take into account the benefits to be gained from
cooperation as opposed to the costs in money and time in
achieving that cooperation.   The goals will vary according to
the size and nature of the collections available and on the
basis of the librarians' estimate of the value of each to the
library's patrons.

Levels of Access

The library staff can then discuss with the managers
of those collections the level of access available to people
outside the immediate interest groups for which the collections
were established. Several levels of access may exist. In the
most restrictive cases, only faculty and staff in the specific
department or unit may be authorized to use a collection. In
a less restrictive situation graduate students in the particular
discipline may also be able to use it. Or all people in the
discipline, including undergraduates, may have access to the
collection. Further degrees of access, which tend to be less
common, extend use to others within the institution or, further
still, to people outside the institution. Clearly any new ex-
tensions of access involve more work for those who maintain
the collection and may result in some inconvenience to the
primary users of the collection. To justify the additional
labor involved, representatives of the main library system
may have to investigate and explain the mutual benefits available to users of these collections and users of the library
system. Librarians could suggest, for example, that the
duplication of little-used expensive materials be eliminated so
that the library and/or the collection could purchase a larger
number of materials in the designated subject field. With
more frequent communication, the library should be able to
select materials more appropriate to the needs of users in
that field.

These discussions will require much diplomacy on the
part of the librarians. Some managers of valuable collections
may have no interest in cooperating with the library. If all
suggestions of voluntary cooperation are rejected, the librarians might consider involving the institution's central administration in an effort to obtain wider access to these collections.
Libraries in some institutions are charged with the specific
responsibility for all books and other information sources acquired by the institution, even though that responsibility may
seldom be enforced. Although the power of such authority,
or pressure from the central administration, might succeed
in forcing some degree of access, such action might also
arouse the antagonism of the managers of the collections involved. Steps of this kind, therefore, should be taken only
as a last resort, and only when the collection is clearly worth
this type of effort.

In general the managers of independent collections may
see any library interest in their materials as the first step

in a move toward annexation.   The disapproval that administrators and staff of official libraries frequently voice about
these independent collections provides some basis for such
apprehensions.   If the library is not interested in taking over
these collections, its representatives should be very careful
in explaining their purpose in order to ensure maximum cooperation without arousing apprehensions or expectations.

     In fact, among the most serious problems for the li-
brary in establishing contact with these collections is that
the managers may expect the library to do more for them
than it can, or is prepared to do.   The library may be offered
donations of a collection's discards to be processed and maintained.   The managers may request acquisitions funds, processing help, or staffing from the library.   The library staff
should recognize and prepare for the possibility of encounter-
ing either hostility or excessive demands before meeting with
these groups.   The staff needs to understand the level of access for each collection that the library has set as a long-
term goal.   If this level is high, the library should consider
suggesting initially intermediate levels to the managers of the
relevant collections.   The staff should decide upon the degree
of help which the library is willing and able to provide before
help is requested, so that if the occasion arises, the library
does not appear to be asking for favors while giving nothing
in return.   Otherwise the library may generate ill will rather
than a good working relationship.

Sharing Information and Resources

     After representatives from the library and other col-
lections have decided on the level of access to those collections which will be allowed, the methods for achieving this
access can be considered.   The most basic step is the compilation of a directory of information resources based on the
survey data.   A directory of that kind can give staff throughout the institution an overview of the range of resources available.   Where access is to be limited, the public service staff
of the library system can use this directory to refer appropriate people to those collections.   In this way the level of
demand placed on a collection can be controlled.

     For collections which will tolerate a broader level of
access, the directory of resources can be distributed more
widely throughout the institution.   This may require more
work for the managers of the independent collection because

some people who could have used the central library materials
will go directly to the outside collection, as will some who
need materials not owned by the central library.   There may
be other problems, too, such as a possible increase in the
incidence of theft or mutilation.   The manager of the independent collection, therefore, may not wish the directory information to be made so widely available.

It is essential that the library staff be certain of the
extent to which information about these collections can be
publicized, and it may be necessary to prepare two listings.
One listing might serve only for internal library staff use,
for collections where access is to be limited, while the other
may be more widely distributed.

Collections of some magnitude might also provide the
library system with a list of the major items in the collection, as well as a general estimate of the kinds and amount
of material included.   Such information can be kept either at
the library's public service desks, or included in brief form
in the directory.

The most convenient method of informing the patron of
the availability of materials in outside collections is by including records describing those materials in the central library's
card catalog with appropriate location indicators.   This method,
of course, entails additional processing and service costs for
both the library system and the outside collection.   Those
costs can be justified most readily when the materials are
not already owned by the library system but are important
to faculty and students in other disciplines in the institution.

If the library and an independent collection wish to
establish a productive working relationship, one aspect of such
a relationship can be the establishment of a formal liaison
between them to exchange information on new acquisitions in
appropriate subject areas.   Such a liaison can alert each to
purchases made by the other.   This can help to avoid unnecessary duplication and can give the library an indication
of what items the users of the independent collection need.

If the budget of an independent collection is substantial,
the collection and the library might even establish a cooperative acquisitions policy.   Representatives of the library and
the collection could then confer before making purchases in
specifically defined subject areas.   Alternatively, the library
and the collection could each take responsibility for purchasing

in different aspects of a discipline so that there will be less
overlap between them.   If the library already has a good
written collection development policy statement, it may be
possible to incorporate into it sections pertaining to the independent collections on campus.   The advantages offered by
a written collection development policy may well be a selling
point the library staff can use in negotiating with the managers
of independent collections.

The most comprehensive levels of access to an outside
collection would entail making all, or some part, of that collection an administrative part of the library system.   The
collection might either remain in its original location or be
moved to a building already within the purview of the central
library system.   Such a procedure is expensive and may, if
the collection is to be moved, require additional space in library buildings.   Contrary to the belief of many librarians,
this comprehensive a level of access may be neither necessary nor desirable.   Unless the collection is quite valuable,
either in terms of its market value or in terms of its informational value for the rest of the community, the undertaking
may be more costly than it is worth.

If the collection is small but valuable, an administrative and physical relocation may be feasible.   The larger the
collection, the less likely it is that the library will have the
space to house it.   Larger collections will also probably already have employees assigned to them.   Some of those employees may be subject specialists and, therefore, able to
provide detailed assistance to users of the collection.   Subject specialists are not likely to be interested in, or capable
of, working in the public or technical services involved in
the broader scope of the central library system.   Finally,
the larger and more established an outside collection is, the
greater the number of people likely to have a vested interest
in the maintenance of the collection as a separate entity.   In
such cases it is probably more useful to let the collection
remain where it is and to seek only to establish a strong organizational link between the library system and the collection.   If the managers of large and valuable collections report administratively to the director of the library system,
then collection development and services can be more easily
coordinated so that the institution will receive the greatest
possible benefit from its materials budget.   Even this link-
age, however, could involve some loss of autonomy for the
managers of the collection, and they may, therefore, resist
it unless it can be demonstrated to have advantages to them.

If the staff of the library system and the managers of the collection cannot reach an agreement as to the appropriate level of cooperation, the institution's central administration may have to become involved. For the sake of future working relationships this level of involvement should probably be avoided if at all possible. Whatever decision is finally reached, it should be one that allows the library and the collection to make the most efficient use of each other's resources.

Implications for the Library System

In addition to increasing staff awareness of additional information resources, and expanding the range of resources available to patrons, such a project can have other benefits for the library system. It can be used as a good means of gaining information about how the main library's collections and services are perceived by the managers and users of independent collections on campus. This can be done by including in the original survey questions that deal with:

+ the similarity of the independent collection's holdings to those in the library
+ the amount of use made of the main library
+ the geographic location of the independent collection in relationship to the library system
+ the reasons for the establishment and maintenance of the independent collection.

If the library perceives a pattern to the responses (i. e., if a number of these independent collections are being created and maintained for similar reasons), the library staff may need to examine and possibly modify its collecting and service policies in order to provide the best level of service possible with available resources.

Conclusion

Given the need to maintain or even expand services in the face of increasing economic constraints, libraries will more and more need information regarding materials within the institution which are not owned by the library system. This information can be obtained by the kind of survey questionnaire that has been described above. The information from such a survey can be used as the basis for various levels of cooperative action ranging from the production of

a directory of information resources on campus to the full
integration of those independent resources into the library
system.   The level of cooperation to be sought should be determined by the size and uniqueness of the collection and by
its value in meeting the institution's informational needs.
Information that can be gained from such a survey about the
purpose of these outside collections can also be very useful
to the library system as a measure of its ability to meet
the needs of the institution.   The possibility of increased access to resources and of obtaining information useful in examining library performance makes the project of surveying
campus information sources and services a worthwhile undertaking.

<u>Note</u>

1.   Genaway, David C. and Edward B. Stanford.   "Quasi-
     departmental Libraries, " <u>College and Research Libraries</u>
     38:187-94, 1977.

PREPARING FOR THE AUTOMATION OF ACQUISITIONS

by Bonnie Naifeh Hill

Abstract

As the automation of the acquisitions function becomes more feasible and more widespread, it is necessary for libraries to pay careful attention to the preliminary steps in developing, or accepting, an automated acquisitions system and to their basic requirements for such a system. This paper outlines the initial planning steps of analyzing procedures, analyzing staff, and determining costs that should be undertaken, and describes the general features of an automated acquisitions system that would seem to be desirable.

Introduction

In the past few years computerized cataloging has become the rule rather than the exception in libraries; computerized circulation systems continue to replace manual systems; and reference departments are making widespread use of on-line bibliographic data bases in order to provide better service to their users. Now the possible automation of acquisitions systems is receiving increasing attention. Several automated turnkey acquisitions systems are being offered; others are in the planning stage; and a number of libraries have adopted, or are developing, a locally automated system for this vital library function.

Acquisitions seems to be an area particularly suited to automation. There are many repetitive tasks which, due to their complex nature, require highly trained workers but are particularly amenable to automation. An automated acquisitions system also holds out the promise of providing greater accuracy at greater speed with less cost, and of providing greater flexibility in the maintenance and manipulation of information than does any manual system.

At present acquisitions departments in most libraries are strained by the need to acquire more materials with fewer dollars, both in terms of reduced book budgets and purchasing power and of increased staff costs. Clearly the pros and cons of automation need to be evaluated seriously before commitments of time and money are made in exploring or adopting a system. A library must know what it is getting into before considering automation of this function.

The purpose of this paper is to suggest an approach to preparing to consider the automation of the acquisitions system within a library in order to help decision-makers arrive at the best possible solution for their individual institutions. It largely focuses on the critical planning stage of the process. That stage is a critical one, for at that time, in addition to carefully analyzing existing procedures, staffing, and costs, a library must attempt to articulate for itself what advantages over a manual system any automated system must offer, what it should offer in the way of extra services, what the library is willing, or able, to expend for an automated system, what trade-offs can be accepted between services and costs, and what the potential impact of an automated system may be on its present acquisitions processes and procedures. The process is not an easy one, and some adjustments and compromises may have to be made; but, with some forethought and planning, the experience can be a positive rather than a negative one.

Analyze Procedures

While it may now seem trite to say so, any consideration of automation must begin with a careful analysis of current practices and procedures. That is certainly true for acquisitions. Indeed, whether or not automation is being considered as an immediate alternative, it is always useful to undertake such an analysis. Perhaps the best way to do this for the acquisitions function is to write, or rewrite, a procedures manual. This can be done by the head of the department, by an ad hoc committee, or by having each person in the department write a statement outlining his/her duties and responsibilities in detail and indicating how they are performed. While the latter approach may be most effective, it requires a careful review and editing of the material by someone who knows and understands the entire process. No matter who does it, the result must be a detailed and comprehensive statement of what the department is doing and

how it is doing it. The scope of the department's functions
must be clearly delineated in such a way as to explain the
parameters within which it functions. It is also essential to
take into account tasks related to the acquisitions function
that may be performed in other departments, to be certain
that a comprehensive picture of the overall acquisitions function is obtained.

Any acquisitions system must identify materials suitable
for inclusion in the collection; establish the bibliographic existence of the material with accuracy; determine whether or
not the material is already in the collection; verify the market availability of the material; decide the best way of obtaining the material; initiate the order; provide information on
material that is on order; allow for the ready matching of
material received in a timely fashion; keep track of the necessary fund accounting; and provide for the payment of in-
voices. In addition to these general requirements, which are
necessary for any system, there are likely to be local or institutional requirements of a fairly specific nature.

A procedures manual, if it is to be useful, must cover
all of those steps, beginning with the question of how the department becomes aware of a possible selection and ending
with the question of how unresolved claims for payment from
vendors are handled. All of the steps must be covered in
detail and the forms used and the records kept at each step
of the way must be spelled out.

As this work is being done, of course, a careful review of the rationale and need for particular steps and procedures should also be conducted. This should be done to
determine both whether certain tasks can be eliminated or
handled more efficiently, and whether other tasks need to be
added to the process. The keeping of statistics and the claiming and vendor analysis procedures are two areas that may
require particular attention. It may be possible to incorporate additional tasks into the acquisitions procedure at this
stage without overburdening staff, but careful thought must be
given as to whether or not that should be done in terms of
the likelihood of actually implementing an automated system
in the near future. There is little point in adding to, or substantially altering, procedures if automation is soon likely to
recast the entire process.

Analyze Staffing

Another essential initial project is an analysis of the levels of staffing involved in performing the various duties and tasks of the acquisitions department. This can be done in elaborate detail, and that may be necessary or desirable, but even a less elaborate analysis can shed much light on the situation. The first step is the articulation of the present situation. Each staff member's tasks should be described in detail and some method of identifying the appropriate level of a task (i. e., clerical, preprofessional, professional) must be established. This process can assist in determining whether staff are performing duties appropriate to their educational background and experience and the level of their assignment. Often, of course, such an analysis will reveal that the professional staff is doing a considerable amount of clerical work.

Improper work activities may be the result of inadequate or improper staffing but, just as often, they may be simply the result of custom. In any case a critical eye must be turned to the results of such a staffing analysis so that the acquisitions librarian can be freed of some of the clerical tasks in order to allow time to perform the ever-increasing professional functions of selection, faculty liaison, and budgetary control.

Just as procedures may need to be changed, so tasks may need to be reassigned, or staffing patterns may need to be altered. Here again, however, the likelihood of adopting an automated system in the near future must be taken into account. Since an automated system should relieve all of the members of the department of tedious and repetitive tasks, any reassignment of duties should consider that eventuality. Those tasks that can be eliminated when an automated system is adopted should be identified; the remaining clerical tasks should be clearly delineated for assignment to clerical staff, and the professional duties clearly delineated for assignment to the professional staff. In particular the number of staff that may be required and the level of each of those staff members should be identified. It is not suggested that this second step of staffing analysis be implemented immediately. Some aspects of it may require immediate attention, and the addition, elimination, or reassignment of staff. In general, this information should be used as the basis for establishing the new staffing patterns required within an automated system.

Before a decision is reached to eliminate or phase out staff, it is important to consider whether or not the present level of departmental performance is, in fact, the desired level. If the situation allows, it may well be worth considering what additional duties, not now performed, could be undertaken by the existing acquisitions staff with the advent of an automated system. With a searching staff trained in the use of the computer and bibliographic searching, for example, retrospective bibliographies could be searched and citation analysis procedures performed in order to gather data which could reveal gaps and strengths in the collection. Data on titles withdrawn or replaced due to loss, theft, or mutilation could be analyzed to provide information about popular areas of the collection that might require more attention. Other analyses of data that would be helpful in improving the performance of the acquisitions department could be undertaken. The desirability, and the possibility, of using staff to accomplish these new functions must be balanced against the costs of an automated system and other demands for staff within the library. It is more than likely that, taking into account the costs of automation, the library will not be able to afford to maintain existing staff levels over a period of time. Even a phasing out of staff, however, must be taken into account so that the most effective use of staff can be made at all times. It may well be possible, for example, to undertake special projects in a transitional period while staff is being phased out because of the lowered staff requirements of an automated system.

Determine Costs

The next stage in the preparatory process, although it may accompany and build on the preceding stages, is the determination of the present costs of the acquisitions operation in as fine a detail as possible. Costs may be analyzed either on the basis of line item costs, or of procedural costs. Line item costs are perhaps a grosser measure of the present costs of the acquisitions functions but may be more than adequate for a general comparison with the costs of an automated system. A line item analysis simply measures all general budgetary costs currently expended as a part of the acquisitions function, including staff, supplies, equipment, travel, postage, overhead, etc. The determination of procedural costs is more difficult and time consuming and may require considerably more effort and expertise. In general, in this approach an effort is made to determine the costs of the individual procedures

identified in a staffing analysis process. That may include
such things as: the cost of searching a title; the cost of preparing an order; the cost of encumbering an account; and the
cost of sending an order.

One decision that must be made at the outset in determining procedural costs is to arrive at a clear definition of
each procedure, determining where one procedure ends and
another begins. It is especially important to define those
procedures in such a way as to allow for a meaningful comparison with the costs of potential automated systems. It is
also important that these procedures be defined in such a way
that they can be readily combined and aggregated. All work
of the department, and related work performed in other departments, should be assigned to one of the procedures and
definitions and, once assigned, should be applied consistently.

Requirements of Automation

Once a procedure manual has been written, staffing
patterns analyzed, and costs determined, the acquisitions department should have the manual system most suited to the
conditions of the institution, should know how that system can
be improved, and should have a reasonably accurate idea of
what it costs. The next step is to develop a carefully prepared list of the requirements of the acquisitions department,
the library, and the institution for an automated system. All
of the features and elements that may be required, or desired,
should be identified, and placed in some kind of priority order. It is essential to have a sound idea of what those requirements are before beginning to examine particular systems, and the development of a written statement of those
needs, even if relatively brief, is a good starting point.

There are, of course, a wide range of requirements
and they are likely to vary considerably from library to library. Several of them, however, are fundamental to any
system and should be considered in this stage of the planning.

One of the primary considerations to be taken into account is the nature and composition of the data base that supports the system. Without such a data base, the scope of an
automated acquisitions system will be severely restricted and
considerable personnel will still be required to maintain an
auxiliary manual searching system. On the other hand, the
process of converting a library's entire shelflist or catalog

into machine-readable form can be a considerable undertaking in time and expense, and it is understandable that many libraries using automated systems have failed to make this conversion. Even with such a conversion the utility of a data base restricted to an institution's own holdings is more limited than one which incorporates external records. But those external records must be in a form that is compatible with other systems used by a library, and with existing acquisitions records, so that the library can make effective use of them. The library's requirements in terms of the content and scope of the data base used to support an acquisitions system must be specifically identified in the planning process.

Those records, no matter what the scope, must provide for identification of an item complete enough to allow the acquisitions process to proceed. Not only author, title, place of publication, publisher, and date of publication are needed. Other necessary information includes price, pagination, physical description, series, LC card number, ISBN or ISSN number, editor, translator, illustrator, edition, number of volumes or parts, distributor, and either publisher's or distributor's address. All of these elements are necessary for the adequate identification of an item and for the work of the selection and order process. They should appear, when applicable, for every item in the data base. Any automated system that offers less than this should be carefully examined for its present and future suitability and adaptability. It would also be helpful to have information about such matters as discounts and title changes incorporated as part of the data base. That information can only come from publishers and jobbers, however, and would require input from them as well as from library sources. While this may be possible, and certainly would be to the advantage of all concerned, it is not likely to occur in the near future except in systems developed and marketed by publishers and jobbers; unfortunately, in other respects those systems may have data bases that are, in general, far less comprehensive than library-based systems. The library must be able to identify its needs and priorities and to know what tradeoffs, if any, it is willing to make in terms of its requirements for particular items of identification within the records of a data base, as opposed to the nature and scope of the data base.

If the information provided is sufficiently comprehensive and in a suitable format, further consideration must be given to the potential for interfacing with other automated systems already functioning in, or planned for, a particular

library. This is not just a question of the ability of systems
to share and transfer appropriate information but may involve
other important considerations such as staff acceptance, the
need for additional training, the need to duplicate records,
and other matters which may have an impact upon cost as
well as effectiveness.

The system must also, of course, be capable of generating the forms necessary to the ordering of the book, and
of maintaining the necessary information relating to that order
until it is no longer needed. Automation, in and of itself,
should greatly simplify this area of operations within an acquisitions department. Since a record of the library's holdings and current orders is maintained within the system, the
need for paper files is likely to be substantially diminished.
There is a major consideration in the decision to do away
almost entirely with paper files. The system must accommodate a record of the order's history leading up to the fulfillment or cancellation of an order, and, in some cases, beyond;
if it does not, some paper files must be maintained. Often
issues arise on an order long after the initial acquisitions
process has ended. Those issues might include such things
as: a title which was not received that is now available
again; which reviews or other sources were used to determine
the selection of a particular title; who recommended or selected a particular title; an imperfect copy is discovered and
needs to be returned to the vendor; and similar problems.
Information of this sort does not appear in the cataloging record, but is essential to the continued good service provided
by an acquisitions department. In addition these kinds of
records, maintained over a period of time, may provide the
data for retrospective studies of buying patterns which can
be used to help predict future conditions and guide future
purchases. In this regard data gathered and analyzed by
computer can be of inestimable value in planning, and can
provide much better information than is possible within a
manual system. Too often computer-based systems offer
more sophisticated management information systems as an
incentive but those capabilities are never fully realized. In
any case the need for a particular item of information must
be examined realistically in terms of how often and for what
purpose that item is used as well as in terms of the library's
ability and willingness to pay for that information. It may,
for example, be cheaper simply to absorb the costs of keeping or replacing a book discovered to be damaged some time
after it has been acquired than to maintain records that would
allow the problem to be resolved.

The access points of the paper files of manual systems
should be continued and improved upon in an automated system. The traditional access points include main entry, title,
vendor, and the library's order number. Additional access
points to be offered by an automated system may include fund
source, requester, language, or country of publication.

Often the acquisitions process may involve the searching of standard bibliographies, out-of-print dealers' catalogs,
or desiderata files. Here again an automated system should
be able to provide additional information and assistance in
dealing with these kinds of records, and the library's needs
for that kind of information must be carefully examined and
weighed. The library may wish to keep a record of bibliographies which have been searched for library ownership in a
fashion that shows which items are owned as well as which
items have been or are to be ordered. A method of providing access to information about books which are currently un-
available for purchase but are wanted may be provided so
that this listing can be matched against the catalogs of out-
of-print dealers and reprinters or against new records being
added to the data base.

Finally, of course, a comprehensive automated acquisitions system should have full accounting and bookkeeping
capabilities. For each order generated the record should
show the date ordered, the amount of money encumbered, the
vendor with whom the order is placed, the fund to which it
is to be charged, and a unique order item number. Once
the item is received the system should be able to generate
the necessary records of verification so that payment can be
made in accordance with established institutional practices.
The system should also allow for cancellations or changes in
orders. Automatic claiming, if the item has not been received within a predetermined specified time period, should
be available, but can perhaps best take the form of generating
a list of claims on a regular basis for review and action by
the acquisitions staff. The production of the necessary financial reporting and accounting records, including detailed fund
accounting, is among the most essential elements of an automated system. Any system must be able to maintain and
supply those records and that accounting and should be able
to do so in accordance with established institutional requirements. That process must allow for the production of full
budget reports on a regular schedule, or on demand, providing information about such things as encumbrances, balances,
fund status, and vendor payments. In particular the ability

of a system to provide information that will allow the library
to analyze in detail the performance of individual vendors in
a number of regards should be carefully considered.

These are some of the basic features of an automated
acquisitions system that most libraries are likely to consider
significant. Each library will no doubt have additional features that it feels are essential to meet its needs. In any
case it is essential that a library articulate its particular
needs and requirements in as much written detail as possible
before beginning to examine and consider particular systems.
To wait until a later point in the review process to identify
and articulate needs may well result in a library's conforming
to a larger extent than necessary to the demands, or limitations, of a particular system rather than being able to insist
that the system accommodate and respond to the library's
needs.

Conclusion

Analyzing procedures and staffing, determining present
costs, and identifying the library's needs are the essential
first steps in consideration of the adoption of an automated
acquisitions system within a library. Once those steps have
been accomplished, a library can then begin to consider and
review the actual alternatives. In acquisitions an increasing
number of possibilities exist and the advantages and disadvantages of each must be carefully weighed. That should be
relatively easy if careful planning has gone into the initial
steps of the process.

The caveats that apply to any major purchase, individual or institution, apply with particular relevance here. Find
out as much as possible about any system being considered,
not just by reading the sales literature and listening to the
salespeople but by examining the system in operation and
talking to staff in libraries that are already using it. Be
careful to try to establish what the system really offers and
to identify how well it meets your pre-established needs, as
opposed to simply considering the implications of what a system offers or being swayed by promises of future modifications.

After examining all alternatives, including the possibility of designing and implementing a local system, the systems should be compared against each other and against the

library's existing manual system in terms of cost, services, staff requirements, etc. If you have done your homework well it should be possible not only to identify which system, if any, meets your needs but to develop a strong justification for its acquisition.

THE ROLE OF THE CORPORATE LIBRARY
IN COOPERATIVE GROUPS

by Dorothy Kijanka

Abstract

The role of corporate libraries in multitype cooperative groups has steadily evolved from informal participation
into the present more complex forms.   Corporate librarians
take a practical approach to cooperation and make serious
efforts to objectively evaluate their participation in cooperative activities.   The obstacles to cooperation and the benefits
to be derived are assessed from the viewpoint of profit and
loss.   Corporate libraries can most effectively participate in
cooperative activities by using a cooperative group as a third-
party agent to act on their behalf.

Introduction

The experience of corporate libraries in cooperative
groups is especially valuable in evaluating such groups because of the nature of corporate library work.   Corporate
librarians operate under the pressures characteristic of profit-
making companies.   Services must pay for themselves or
make a profit if they are not to be eliminated.   In such an
environment librarians may very well lose their jobs if they
are not cost-conscious.   Corporate librarians, therefore, tend
to take a hard-nosed, practical approach to cooperation because they must prove to their management that such cooperation will pay.   Working under this kind of pressure leads
them to become impatient with only promises of better service through cooperative groups.   They must be shown that
a cooperative group can indeed supplement an existing communications system which may have satisfied their needs for
many years.

Because corporate libraries have profit-making companies

as parent institutions, they were once considered to be independent and self-centered, and, therefore, out of the main-
stream of the library world.   The assumption was that money
was always available; corporate libraries seemed to be the
first to accept new ideas and to purchase and use new equipment to meet specific needs.   In reality, corporate librarians
have always been cost-conscious and very practical in their
attitude toward their work.   Although they may have had access to funding somewhat more readily than publicly supported
libraries, they have had to prove that the money was being
spent wisely.   This emphasis on practicality, together with
the high degree of motivation which leads corporate librarians
to seek out information wherever it may be found, are the
two major influences on the participation of corporate librarians in cooperative groups.

       Cooperative groups representing all types of libraries
are emerging as the dominant means of cooperation, on the
premise that no one library can satisfy the needs of its users,
that different types of libraries have a diversity of resources,
and that users should have access to all library resources.
Efforts to bring different kinds of libraries together are increasingly encouraged by the professional associations and
national planning activities, and in many cases are authorized
by state legislation and funding. [1]   The benefits and problems
associated with multitype cooperative efforts may both be
more pronounced in proportion to the number and types of
libraries participating.   Before many libraries are able to
adjust to cooperation with similar libraries, they are asked
to enter into new relationships with institutions with which
they may have no common interest except in providing information to users.   Corporate libraries, especially, seem to
have less in common with other types of libraries.   The
history of corporate library participation in cooperative efforts, however, indicates that corporate libraries have always
been willing to cooperate in sharing resources.   The attitudes
of corporate librarians toward cooperation, the problems they
encounter, and the benefits they realize in their relationships
with other libraries, including those in non-profit institutions,
are some of the factors that must be taken into account in
determining the way that such libraries may effectively participate in a cooperative group.

History and Background

       Corporate libraries have a long history of cooperation,

reaching as far back as the creation of the Special Libraries
Association in 1909.   At its first meeting that year, the Association resolved "to unite along cooperative lines, by interchange of ideas, by publication of bibliographies, by circulation of bulletins, and ... by establishing ... a clearinghouse
for answering inquiries arising among various members. "[2]
Special Libraries, the Association's Journal, reported on the
organization's "hope to unite in cooperation all small libraries
through the country; financial, commercial, scientific, indus-
trial; and special departments of state, college and general
libraries. "[3]

        Among the earliest evidence of special library coopera-
tion was a directory of special libraries which appeared in a
1910 issue of Special Libraries.   Many national, regional,
and local directories have been published since that time.
The first cooperative ventures were sponsored by the Special
Libraries Association and were carried out by libraries with
a common subject interest or geographic location.   Interlibrary lending and reciprocal use of collections were the primary means of cooperation.   There was an early and continued emphasis on the publication of union lists of periodicals
due to the importance of journals as a principal resource in
corporate libraries.   Plans were made for projects in the
fields of cooperative cataloging, storage centers, cooperative
acquisitions, and duplicate exchange.   These cooperative efforts were usually among those special libraries with similar
interests.

        An excellent recent overview of corporate and other
kinds of special libraries is found in a report prepared for
the National Advisory Commission on Libraries.   The report
includes several background papers on the definition and
state-of-the-art of special librarianship, the results of a survey of the major problems and contributing potentials of these
libraries to cooperative schemes, and recommendations for
future action. [4] Definitive articles have also appeared in issues of Library Trends devoted to cooperation and in Library
Quarterly. [5]

        Special Libraries, the journal of the Special Libraries
Association, continues to contain a wide range of articles on
the subject of cooperation.   The journal is valuable for providing a forum in which the different viewpoints on cooperation
are debated.   Here can be found all the usual arguments for
or against cooperation.   The approach that many corporate
librarians take, however, shows a more open and outspoken

pursuit of their own interests. In the April 1964 issue of
Special Libraries, Kay Daniels and Charles Nelson, of the
management consulting firm of Nelson Associates, presented
a defense of the concept of self-interest. They contended
that a librarian whose first responsibility is to his own institution might render a disservice to the institution if he un-
critically attempted to meet all requests from other sources.
They felt that all cooperative ventures should undergo a test-
ing period and that

> Objective appraisal of the results of any cooperative
> program is of critical importance, for just as it
> may be frivolous to initiate a cooperative program
> for its own sake, it is unrealistic to continue with
> one if it does not serve the interests of the cooper-
> ating libraries. [6]

Guidelines to Cooperation

        Discussion on the merits of cooperation continues, but
to bring some order to the field in 1977 the Special Libraries
Association issued a set of guidelines to help librarians to decide whether they should cooperate and how to go about it. [7]
One of the first decisions to be made is whether to join an
existing cooperative group or to form a new one.   This decision should be made during what is called the exploratory
phase.   This phase should begin with the study and discussion
of the basic concepts of formal cooperation.   The guidelines
suggest that a review of the literature be made and that a
small group of librarians meet to share their ideas and understanding of this kind of formal cooperation.

        The next step during the exploratory phase is for a
librarian to consider his/her library in relationship to the
state of cooperation.   This is the point at which a librarian
should ask, "What's in it for me?" and, at the same time,
"What can my library contribute?"   If the answers are negative it is assumed that the subject should not be pursued
further.   Those who wish to make a commitment will take
the next step of exploring existing cooperative groups which
might be joined, and deciding whether to join an existing
group, create a new one, or both.   It is possible that participation in several groups will be necessary to fulfill all
needs.

        Further steps in the exploratory phase are taken with

the decision to create a new group. Potential members, librarians with similar interests, should be identified and gathered together. The guidelines suggest that the group be given
a name before detailed planning is begun. This helps to identify the cooperative group clearly in the minds of members.

   The planning and development phase of establishing the
group begins with identification of objectives. The guidelines
recommend that the objectives be realistic and that practical
goals be set. Suggestions and examples are given for an organizational structure and the drafting of bylaws and tentative
program plans. The development phase ends with a plan for
funding, the appointment of a director of the cooperative group,
and the location of office space for group headquarters.

   Evaluation is considered an important element in the
operational phase of the group. The guidelines call for a
detailed design of short-range activities which includes basic
policies and evaluation procedures. Each activity should be
implemented and evaluated on a trial basis. Progress reports
should be made to everyone concerned with the cooperative
group, including member institutions, governing board, staff,
and funding sources. If the evaluation calls for it, design
and policy modifications should be made. Long-range plans
can then be developed. The guidelines recommend that evaluation be an ongoing procedure in all activities and that the
membership be deeply involved in the planning and evaluation
process.

   Reflected throughout the guidelines is a concern that
each librarian become aware of what cooperation involves,
and that this knowledge be used to make objective decisions.
Although the makers of the guidelines assume that the decision
to participate is made during the exploratory phase, it is evident that a decision to withdraw can be made at any number
of later stages in the process. The guidelines provide a clear
and concise picture of what steps are necessary to form a cooperative group. They do not give the answers to the questions of what is gained or contributed by participation in a
group, but they do suggest ways in which these answers may
be found.

   The guidelines make the process of joining or creating
a new cooperative group seem effortless. In reality, the experience can represent much hard work and difficult compro-
mise, as most librarians who have been through the process
will testify.

Library Group of Southwestern Connecticut: An Example

It is almost impossible today to be a librarian and not
take part in some cooperative activity between libraries. My
experience in several cooperative groups, especially in one
composed mainly of corporate libraries, has enabled me to
see at first-hand the way in which these groups function. Extensive reading of the literature on cooperation reinforces the
belief that the experience of any local group for the most part
can be accepted as representative of similar cooperative efforts. The history of the Library Group of Southwestern Connecticut appears to be typical of the creation, organization,
and functioning of similar groups elsewhere. The observations in this paper on the role of corporate libraries in cooperative library activities are based to a great extent on my
experience with the Library Group over a period of several
years, during one of which I was its president.

In 1957 a small group of corporate librarians held a
series of informal meetings in Stamford, Connecticut, with
the staff of the business and technology department of the
Ferguson Library, a large urban public library. The purpose
of the meeting was to explore ways in which resources could
be shared. From this beginning the group evolved into a
more formal organization incorporated in 1964 as the Library
Group of Southwestern Connecticut, Inc. Officers were elected
and membership dues assessed. Most of the dues were used
to purchase expensive reference materials or back files of
periodicals which were stored in the Ferguson Library and
made available to all members. Other major projects were
the publication of a directory of members, with a summary
of specialized subject strengths available in each library; the
underwriting of a part of the expenses of special meetings or
workshops for members who otherwise could not attend; an
interlibrary loan program, and a union list of the periodical
holdings of member libraries. Business and program meetings were held several times a year, and a major workshop
annually. Most of the work was done voluntarily by member
librarians; no funds were available for a paid staff. Much
of the cost of major projects, such as for the computer time
involved in the production of the union list, was absorbed by
the member libraries. As the organization grew its membership expanded to include representation from other types of
libraries. A few public, academic, and school libraries, as
well as other types of special libraries, such as law and
hospital libraries, joined the group.

Although the Library Group of Southwestern Connecticut functioned satisfactorily on a relatively informal basis for many years, it eventually felt the need for a more formal organization to achieve its goals. As it became more difficult to carry out major projects, the Library Group saw the need for a paid administrative staff and some means of financing the projects other than with grants or voluntary contributions. A fee schedule based on services rendered was seen as one solution, but creating an organization along these lines would have been difficult without the initial availability of substantial financial resources.

At the same time that the Library Group of Southwestern Connecticut began to feel the need for more formal cooperation, the library community in the state of Connecticut was moving toward the same goal. In 1975 the state legislature authorized the creation of a Criteria Review Board which was to set criteria for and to encourage the formation of Cooperating Library Service Units (CLSU's) in different sections of the state. The CLSU's were to be organizations of different types of libraries in given areas of the state whose purpose was to improve library service through cooperation. CLSU's were to promote improved library service through coordinated planning, resource-sharing, and the design, on a regional basis, of services too costly or too impractical at the local level. The state was divided into six regions for the purpose of library cooperation and the sum of $50,000 was to be made available to each region for the first year after it has organized into a cooperating library service unit.

One of the criteria established for the creation of the CLSU's was that only one organization could be the official representative of a region and be eligible to receive state funding. In addition, the organization had to represent all types of libraries. Since the region in which the Library Group of Southwestern Connecticut was located already had two other cooperative groups, it was necessary to form a new organization with members from those groups as well as from libraries not previously represented by any group, such as school libraries and historical societies.

Integrating the various interests represented by different types of libraries was difficult during the formative period of the new organization. Many members of the Library Group of Southwestern Connecticut were reluctant to abandon an organization in which they felt comfortable for one which

has not yet proven itself.   At the same time, they realized
that the kind of library service they wished to provide might
not be possible unless they participated in the new organization. Other members of the Library Group of Southwestern
Connecticut felt that their needs were being adequately met
by the existing organization.

In the end, members were forced to choose between
the two organizations since they either could not afford to
belong to both or saw no need to have duplicate memberships.
Although funded primarily by the state, the new organization
planned to use those funds for administrative purposes, and
instituted membership fees to pay for projects. As the majority of corporate libraries saw the future of cooperation in
the new organization, especially in light of continued state
funding, the Library Group of Southwestern Connecticut voted
to disband and turn its assets over to the new group, the
Southwestern Connecticut Library Council.

At the time of its dissolution, the membership of the
Library Group of Southwestern Connecticut was made up of
forty-one corporate libraries, thirteen public libraries, four
academic libraries, one high school library, and six special
libraries of other types. In spite of the participation of different types of libraries, the activities of the group had always been focused largely on corporate library interests.
With the dissolution of the Library Group of Southwestern
Connecticut, these libraries made the transition to the new
group more easily than some other corporate members, who
entered a new, difficult period of adjustment with a larger
number of libraries of all types.

Obstacles to Cooperation

Many obstacles to cooperation which are cited by special librarians are not unique to them, and have appeared
whenever cooperation between other types of libraries is discussed. Small libraries, more than any other kind, should
be able to benefit from cooperation. In reality they may not
be able to benefit at all. Many corporate libraries are small
operations with only one or two staff members who cannot
handle the volume of work created by participation in a cooperative group, and they often cannot afford membership dues
or fees. On the other hand, users' perception of their needs
and of the library service necessary to meet those needs are
a major influence on the development of a library. A corporate

librarian may be more successful than other librarians in altering those perceptions. Only one or two key people in management need to be made aware of the potential of library service, rather than, for example, the diverse elements governing a public library. The problem of the small library, however, is a continuing one and has no easy solution. This is one of the areas in which the influence of the cooperative group can be brought to bear on the management of the small library to make it aware of the levels of service available through participation in the group.

Another problem common to many cooperative groups, and evident in some relationships in the Library Group of Southwestern Connecticut, is what is considered an abuse of the cooperative process. Because of their small size and proprietary holdings, corporate libraries are especially sensitive to this problem. They feel that other librarians, primarily in the public sector, do not properly screen interlibrary loan requests before sending them. They accuse other libraries of sending requests for widely held material to corporate libraries while the corporate libraries feel they should be used only as a last resort for unique material. The same complaint is made about reference requests. Corporate libraries argue that patrons of other libraries are encouraged to contact them directly, and that this violates agreed-upon procedures.

Some corporations, on the other hand, are accused of maintaining no resources at all, and of using, instead, outside libraries to meet all their needs. The practice of relying on other libraries' collections instead of developing one's own is seen as a major abuse only if no attempt is made to purchase materials. Because of tight budgets librarians are predisposed to supply materials to libraries with financial difficulties. All libraries are expected to develop their own collections rather than using a cooperative group as if it were their only resource. A highly organized cooperative group may be able to correct some of these abuses by screening requests and acting as a third party. It is not always possible, however, to prevent librarians or patrons from going directly to a source when they know it exists and can get needed information in that way more quickly.

The bibliographical standardization required by networks is difficult for corporate libraries to meet. Because their collections are made up of unusual materials, their methods of organizing the collections may also be unusual. A classi-

fication system may have been created to meet the requirements of unique material and might not be used by any other
library. This problem is especially noticeable in the creation
of union lists and catalogs, one of the bases on which any cooperative group should be formed.

          Librarians who have received professional training are
generally aware of the relationship of their library to other
libraries of varying sizes and types. Corporate librarians
who may have attained their positions without training or previous library experience have a handicap that is difficult to
overcome. Professionally trained librarians have a knowledge
and awareness of librarianship that their untrained colleagues
may achieve only after long experience if at all. The lack
of a background in librarianship prevents many librarians
from providing adequate services or fulfilling the needs of
their users. Whatever else formal education for librarianship
does, it provides an awareness of the options open to a working librarian. The knowledge that several kinds of circulation
systems exist, for example, can save much time and effort
which might have been spent in researching circulation systems. This principle can be extended to the field of cooperation. A librarian who is aware of the kinds of cooperative
activities available which can improve services has a distinct
advantage when trying to satisfy users' needs.

          The perception of needs and of the quality of library
service is to some extent personal, especially for librarians
who may not have a library degree or who may have had very
little contact with the profession. Many corporate librarians
work alone, some even without clerical assistance. Often in
such cases the library started as a collection of materials
gathered by various staff members and became large enough
to require at least part-time control. Rather than hire a librarian, the management of the corporation would transfer a
secretary or clerical worker, or perhaps a Ph.D. whose
services were no longer required on the research staff.
These "instant librarians" came with a wide variety of back-
grounds. Some of them became interested enough in their
work to want to learn more about libraries. They either
went to library school or approached their local cooperative
group for assistance in developing a library. Although excellent libraries sometimes emerged from such small beginnings,
in many cases the library remained merely a collection of
materials.

          In instances when a corporation recognizes the need for

a library and wants the best available, professional librarians may be hired with instructions to set up the proper facilities. Again, local cooperative groups can be of assistance by making known the resources already available in the region to which the new library will have access.

But even with the professional library degree, corporate librarians may lack the proper training. The report on special libraries to the National Advisory Commission on Libraries expressed concern over the wide variety in quality of the education and training of special librarians. It recommended that library schools expand their programs to meet the training needs of special librarians, and that library education emphasize the managerial aspects of librarianship. Most library schools do not prepare students to become top administrators upon graduation. Corporate librarians often begin their careers as head librarians and it is important for them to receive managerial and administrative training before assuming such positions. By incorporating this kind of library training with a background and education in special subject materials, corporate librarians can be more effective in providing library service to their specialized clientele.

Expertise in a subject speciality cannot be overlooked. One of the important characteristics of special librarians is the high level of service expected from them, which leads them to conduct exhaustive literature searches and to write reports on the searches for their users. Very rarely do public, academic, or school librarians perform this kind of intensive service. In most cases, a thorough knowledge of the subject is required. Although the desire to seek out the information necessary to provide this level of service wherever it may be found predisposes corporate librarians to join formal cooperative groups, it may also lead to unrealistic expectations of the levels of service provided by other types of libraries.

The question of fees has become a hotly debated topic in libraries, particularly in publicly supported institutions. Corporate librarians have no qualms about paying for services. Their profit-oriented parent organizations are accustomed to paying for services and are therefore willing to pay for library service if it can be demonstrated that the company will benefit. Public libraries, however, may be as reluctant to accept payment from corporations as they are to charge their other users.

Urban public libraries often have special collections
geared to only one part of their public. In an area such as
Southwestern Connecticut, which has a high concentration of
corporate headquarters of national and international business
firms, large public libraries have long felt an obligation to
meet some of the companies' needs for materials. As noted
earlier, it was the interaction between the public and corporate
libraries which formed the basis of the first cooperative group
in the area. As librarians became more aware of the need
to serve all of their public rather than just an elite minority,
the question of allocation of funds became more important.
Although fees can be charged to offset costs of special services, an argument can be made that efforts directed toward
providing special services preclude the establishment of other
needed services. In addition, many library users are unable
to pay for any services even though they might benefit from
them. In spite of the debate on fees, some cooperative groups
currently try to distinguish among the kinds of service corporate libraries may receive by the prorating of membership
dues and the imposition of special fees. The concern over
the charging of fees for special services by public libraries
may be relieved if a third-party agent provides such services.
In addition to establishing programs based on common concerns of all libraries such as reference and interlibrary loan,
the provision of special fee-based services for a variety of
interest groups can be a major incentive for libraries to join
a multi-type cooperative library group.

There is a continuing controversy among corporate
librarians as to the importance of the threat, posed by participation in a cooperative group, to the security of proprietary
information held by their libraries. Some firms work under
government contracts and are required to maintain secrecy.
Other firms are engaged in research directed to the marketing
of a product at a profit. A pharmaceutical firm working on
a new aspirin or toothpaste, for example, does not want its
competitors to know that such research is in progress. They
feel that making their holdings generally known, especially
new acquisitions, might enable competitors to learn about
their current research and future plans. Many librarians
feel that such problems would rarely arise in practice. Others
feel that the threat is serious enough to prevent them from
joining a cooperative group. They prefer to rely on informal
contacts to obtain needed material. By spreading their requests among numerous libraries they protect the privacy of
their company's interests.

Recommendation

     The problems encountered by corporate libraries in their efforts to function with other libraries can be alleviated by participation in a formal cooperative group which acts as a third-party agent. The presence of the agent provides an objective and more efficient means for libraries to deal with one another.

     Small libraries benefit by having the resources of the group available to them without having to spend time searching for locations. The cooperative group also provides a service of particular importance to small libraries by channeling requests so that no one library is unduly burdened. Workshops, training sessions, and other educational functions provided by a cooperative group are valuable not only to the staff of a small library but also to the management of the corporation, which can be made aware of ways in which library service can be improved. As small libraries are often staffed by only one person, the opportunity provided by a cooperative group for librarians to meet should not be ignored. In a survey of attitudes on cooperation of corporate librarian members of the Library Group of Southwestern Connecticut, the interaction between professionals was considered an important benefit. The ability to meet and discuss mutual problems, to hear fresh ideas, to learn of improvements in technology, is as beneficial as learning of new sources of materials.

     Small libraries often find it difficult to contribute to a cooperative group. Generally the only way they can provide service is through the uniqueness of their holdings. If the cooperative group properly performs its function as a third-party agent by channeling requests only for unique holdings, the small library can be a valuable resource for users doing specialized research. Fears that they will be inundated with requests will be relieved once it is demonstrated that a cooperative group can prevent abuses of the interlibrary loan or reference system.

     The problem of bibliographic standardization is not easily solved. Corporate libraries, unlike public and academic libraries, have few or no systems in common. Much of the material in corporate libraries is not in journal or monograph form and many different systems have evolved to cope with the unique material. Many special librarians do

not have the specialized library background which would enable them to catalog material to such standards. This is an
area in which more work needs to be done, and one in which
the cooperative group as third-party agent may be able to
perform or coordinate research on behalf of its members.

The educational function of cooperative groups has already been mentioned, especially with regard to its value for
librarians who are not professionally trained. In many instances, cooperative groups are able to provide opportunities
for training at less cost to their members. Data base vendors, for example, have lower fees for training for groups.
Group member librarians who have expertise in certain fields
often donate their services for training other members. More
effective workshops can be produced because cooperative groups
can also pool their resources to secure experts from outside
the group. The cooperative group performs a valuable function in educating its members in good library service and in
providing the means by which good service can be obtained.

One of the most important functions a cooperative group
can perform is the provision of fee-based services at a cost
less than what would be to an individual library. Automated
data bases, for example, become feasible if several libraries
share the cost. Corporate libraries are often induced to join
a group because of the special fee-based services it provides.
They have always been willing to pay for such services when
available. The ethical or moral considerations disturbing to
non-profit institutions do not arise in a profit-oriented organization. The cooperative group can lift the ethical burden from
the non-profit institutions by providing fee-based services to
libraries or users willing to pay.

Many corporate librarians prefer to use a third-party
agent, such as the paid staff of a cooperative group, to protect their proprietary interests. The staff of a cooperative
group can map out search strategies which spread out requests
over a wide area so that no individual library is aware of
another's interests. The question of the security of information held in one central file is debatable. It may be assumed
that no research is private once information concerning it
leaves the holding library. On the other hand, an assumption
can also be made that the paid staff of a cooperative group
is trustworthy. Usually it is the general dissemination of
holdings information that is objected to, as opposed to controlled distribution which would be provided by a third party.

Conclusion

Although the process of joining or creating a new cooperative group can be a harrowing experience, the group provides a means of dealing rationally with problems in library
relationships that may arise in an emotion-charged atmosphere.
Librarians need this kind of assistance when they meet to discuss the pursuit of their common interests and accommodation
of their special interests.   Any librarian who has taken part
in this process knows that it is extremely difficult.   Even,
or perhaps especially, in cooperative groups that "just grew,"
the various interest groups struggle to maintain their positions.
As new members join a group they bring new interests, perhaps a different concept of cooperation, and varying degrees
and kinds of experience in cooperative groups.   Flexibility of
the group is important.   A librarian who has had negative
experiences in cooperation may be cynical about the possibility
of real progress, while someone with no failures to influence
him may set unrealistic goals.   The interplay of interests, of
ideas and personalities, is a basic part of cooperative activities.   Corporate librarians, noted for their clear-headed approach to problems, can make a valuable contribution to the
success of cooperative groups.

Cooperative groups can bring corporate libraries into
their programs by taking steps to overcome the objections
that those libraries have.   The most effective way to do this
is for the cooperative group to act as a third-party agent between libraries.   Corporate libraries have always been willing
to pay for services and welcome the opportunity to participate
in cooperative groups on this basis if the services are cost-
effective.   Within a group, a library need deal with only one
central office to obtain various services, rather than with
many different libraries, as would otherwise be the case.
This is more efficient and puts the relationship on a business-
like basis, one with which corporate librarians may feel more
comfortable.

If adequately funded and utilized, a third-party agent
can provide all the services required by a library from outside its own resources.   By making arrangements with other
libraries and networks of libraries, the local agent can save
the individual library much time and effort and enable it to
provide better service to its clientele.   The cooperative group
as agent assumes the role of broker or vendor of services and
can act as a clearinghouse of information on library services

for its members. In this way the cooperative group performs
a valuable service to libraries, which in turn can provide
better service to users.

Notes

1. Hamilton, Beth A. and William B. Ernst, Jr. eds.
   Multitype Library Cooperation. New York/London: Bowker, 1977.

2. Woods, Bill. "Regional and National Coordinating and
   Planning for Library Service to Industry, " Library Trends
   14:295-305, 1966.

3. Woods, Bill. "The Potential for Special Libraries in
   Cooperative Ventures for Sharing Library Resources, "
   in Special Libraries, Problems and Cooperative Potentials. Prepared for the National Advisory Commission
   on Libraries. Final Report. Washington, D. C. : American Documentation Institute, 1967.

4. Havlik, Robert J. and others. Special Libraries, Problems and Cooperative Potentials. Prepared for the National Advisory Commission on Libraries. Final Report.
   Washington, D. C. : American Documentation Institute,
   1967.

5. Budington, William S. "Interrelations Among Special
   Libraries, " Library Quarterly 39:64-77, 1969.

6. Daniels, Kay and Charles A. Nelson. "Self-Interest:
   The Test of the Virtue of Cooperation, " Special Libraries
   55:225-6, 1964.

7. Special Libraries Association. Networking Committee.
   Guidelines Subcommittee. Getting into Networking:
   Guidelines for Special Libraries. (SLA State-of-the-Art
   Review No. 5.) New York: Special Libraries Associa-
   tion, 1977.

ACADEMIC LIBRARIANS AND THE
PEER EVALUATION PROCESS

by Louise S. Sherby

Abstract

Based in part on a brief description of elements of the process as used in libraries at Central Washington State College, Rhode Island College, Southern Illinois and Texas A & M, this paper presents a general overview of the peer evaluation process in academic libraries. The need for academic libraries to develop such a process based on criteria appropriate to the special skills and expertise of librarians as faculty members is considered. Also discussed are some of the advantages, problems, and some of the responsibilities inherent in a peer review process.

Introduction

As more and more academic librarians are granted faculty status, many have found that along with this new status come activities and responsibilities not previously encountered. For one, these librarians suddenly find themselves faced with totally new criteria to be used in a new evaluation process similar to those used by the teaching faculty: peer evaluation. As the "Statement on Faculty Status of College and University Librarians" indicates, academic librarians "must go through the same process of evaluation and meet the same standards as other faculty members. "[1]

Often librarians in academic institutions find themselves thrust into doing peer evaluations to satisfy the requirements for evaluation as set down by the college or university administration and/or a collective bargaining agreement. In other instances, even though it is not required, library faculty take peer review upon themselves in an effort to emulate the faculty and to follow the traditional procedures as accepted in a

collegial setting. It also provides the library with a way to
strengthen the nature and quality of the recommendations that
the library makes in the review process by allowing librarians
to have something to say about their peers' performance. The
most important reason for peer evaluation, however, is that
it brings the responsibility for the performance of the professional staff back where it belongs--to the professional staff.
One of the most significant contributions peer review can make
is in influencing and, one hopes, strengthening the professional performance of one's peers and, through them, influencing
the performance of the library as a whole.

       Unfortunately, most academic peer review processes
are designed for evaluation of the teaching faculty. Very
little appears in the literature that attempts to relate the
criteria used for faculty to the work of the academic librarian, with the exception of McAnally's article reinterpreting
those criteria in library terms. [2] While some work has been
done at individual institutions, it is now time for us to begin
to explore in a broader perspective more appropriate criteria
and methods of evaluation for librarians.

Present Practices

       In many institutions the process consists of appointing
or electing a small Personnel Review Committee. Each library faculty member then fills out a written evaluation form
on every other library faculty member, and these forms are
then submitted to the Personnel Review Committee. The
Committee reviews all of the forms and may ask for additional supporting documentation for those faculty being considered
for promotion or tenure. If necessary, appropriate faculty
members may be interviewed, including the member being
evaluated. The Committee makes its recommendations to the
Director of the Library who then forwards them with his own
recommendations, which may not be the same, to the appropriate academic officer.

       In many cases the forms used, however, tend to be
similar, if not identical, to those used for teaching faculty.
Such forms tend to be inadequate and inappropriate for use
in the evaluation of librarians. They are based on criteria
used for the evaluation of the classroom faculty and tend to
emphasize research, publication and service, with some attention to teaching. This may be appropriate for the teaching
faculty but it does not help the librarian whose basic element

of performance is work-related.   These aspects of performance tend to be ignored.   Similarily, because of the work-
load of the librarian (e. g. , the need for staff at all public
service points when the library is open), the librarian is at
an immediate disadvantage in trying to fulfill requirements
for research, publication, etc.   At the same time, the importance of their primary responsibility appears to be down-
graded on the official college or university form.   The time
has not yet come in most institutions when library faculty can
adjust their schedules to allow them to pursue research and
writing activities as part of the 35-hour work week.   Consequently, the library faculty may be expected to perform well
on the job and also perform well in the activities they will be
evaluated on, such as research, publication and service to
the community.   If librarians perform well only on the job,
and do less well at the other activities, they may find that
promotion and tenure decisions will not be in their favor.
For that reason many academic librarians are now developing
criteria related to the practice of librarianship and evaluation
forms which reflect those criteria.   Texas A & M, Central
Washington State College and Southern Illinois University at
Carbondale are a few institutions that have done this.

At Texas A & M, the librarians wanted a system of
evaluation that would "provide insofar as possible--clear,
comprehensible and consistent documentation of the professional growth and performance of librarians. "[3]   The criteria suggested were grouped into "four major categories: job performance, interpersonal relations, professional development,
and service outside the library. "[4]   After presentation to the
faculty of draft forms, a more time-consuming essay form
was chosen as the vehicle for evaluation because it provided
more information about the individual.   An important part of
the form is the Inventory of Professional Service and Growth
which allows the faculty member being evaluated ample opportunity to participate directly in his own evaluation.

The Central Washington State College Library faculty
has developed a checklist rating form on which faculty members are evaluated on a scale of 1 to 9 on six criteria.   There
is also an option for "no basis for judgment. "   Their criteria
range from teaching and/or professional effectiveness, to personal qualities, to professional activities and public service.
Space is provided on the reverse side of the form if the eval-
uator wishes to make additional comments. [5]

The form adopted at Southern Illinois University is

primarily a checklist format but it is more extensive than the
one used at Central Washington.   The form covers all possibilities, so that the instructions can vary according to whether
a supervisor is evaluating a faculty member, a faculty member is evaluating a department head or a non-supervisor faculty member is evaluating a fellow non-supervisor faculty
member. There is an optional self-evaluation section that
can be worked on and completed with one's supervisor. There
are sections for additional comments, if needed, by the eval-
uator. Although not an element of peer evaluation, one innovative section of the form includes a classroom evaluation
form, to be filled out by the student, for those librarians who
have teaching assignments. 6

     Another form of peer evaluation is exemplified by that
used at Rhode Island College: the peer review by discussion.
All faculty, including librarians, are required to fill out a
Personal Data Form annually. That form, which serves as
the basis for all discussion, is a listing of an individual's
achievements in various categories such as education, publications, professional memberships, etc. Supporting documentation can also be submitted to the Departmental Advisory Committee. This Committee then discusses each faculty member
in the presence of the Chairman of the Department, or the
Director of the Library, and makes its recommendations.
This Committee is only advisory and the Chairman, or Director, has the option of making different recommendations, but
must report the Committee's actions. The Chairman, or
Director, writes up a short narrative statement, and recommendation for each person, with the faculty member involved,
before forwarding it to the Vice President for Academic Affairs. The Committee itself submits no written statement,
other than a summary record of action taken, to the Director.

     After working with the college form for several years,
the librarians realized that all that was available was factual
data and that more critical information was needed for effective evaluation of a person's performance. Even though each
faculty member was permitted to make an oral statement to
the Committee prior to its discussion, that option had rarely
been taken advantage of. Originally, most staff felt uncom-
fortable with promoting their own performance and perhaps
felt that other library staff, in a small library, could be
trusted to recognize and comment honestly upon the effectiveness, or lack of effectiveness, of a person's performance.
It was eventually recognized, however, that even in a small
library informal procedures were not necessarily effective.

Therefore a second form was developed, to be used only within the library, to provide the Committee with more substantive information. It is composed of four essay questions and enables each librarian to explain in more detail the activities listed on the college form. This essay form allows each librarian who is being evaluated a much greater opportunity to participate in his/her own evaluation. After three years of use of the two forms, the library faculty has found the original purpose of the second form to be fulfilled. The Committee has additional information, the librarians have more direct input into their own evaluation, and the resulting evaluations seem to be more effective and more directly related to a person's actual job performance.

The Peer Evaluation Process

While there are many forms of peer review, when developing any form of that peer evaluation process there are a number of important points to keep in mind. The first, and most important, is the reason for the entire process. It should be to provide an effective means of evaluating the job performance of the individual library faculty member. Although those performance evaluations may be done for a variety of reasons (e.g., promotion, salary increase, etc.), the main reason should be to provide the person being evaluated with a continuing record of the progress he/she has made, with regard to personal expectations as well as the expectations of colleagues and supervisors.

Obviously peer review, like any other form of evaluation, can be a very subjective process. It is important, therefore, to develop a process that provides for everyone to be evaluated as objectively as possible. An initial step that can be taken is the development of a job description for each member of the library faculty. Such a description enables all staff members to know what each should be doing and, more importantly, allows the individual library faculty member to know what he or she should be doing. The job description should be clearly written and as detailed as necessary but still should allow for a certain degree of flexibility. Preferably, it should be written by both the librarian and his/her supervisor and subject to change by either as the demands of the job change. A job description by itself tends to describe primarily what a person should be doing and, in and of itself, may tell little about what that person has been doing or how well he/she has been doing. A second

step that can be taken is to develop a system of performance
evaluation based on the establishment of specific goals and
objectives by the individual, with advice and direction from
the supervisor, and perhaps even his/her peers. Those goals
and objectives can subsequently be reviewed to determine what
the individual has accomplished. In this way, each librarian
knows what is expected and can gauge more accurately how
well he/she is fulfilling his/her own and the supervisor's expectations and goals. Job descriptions and performance evaluation can also provide the objective base needed for the beginning of the peer review.

Next, general criteria need to be developed that apply
to the special skills and expertise of librarians as faculty
members. Frequently the library faculty are forced to use
criteria already established for the classroom faculty which,
as has been indicated, do not take into account the special
skills of librarianship and, therefore, are difficult to apply
fairly and equitably. If this is the case, then the library
faculty as a group should seek to re-interpret those criteria
in such a way as to retain the intent but to apply them more
meaningfully to the library faculty, or should develop new
criteria specifically for the library faculty. The faculty
should then present the revised or new criteria to the library
and the college or university administration for approval. If
the approach is, for some reason, not accepted by the administration, then the library faculty as a whole must meet and
discuss how and in what manner the criteria for teaching faculty will be applied to the library faculty. Everyone should
participate in this discussion so that all have the same understanding of the criteria and how they will be used in the evaluation process. Whether the criteria used are specific to
the library or are institution-wide, they should be reviewed
annually by the library faculty to ensure that they remain appropriate as changes in the working environment occur.

Another important consideration is the need to develop
an adequate balance between maintaining appropriate safeguards over the confidentiality of information and, at the same
time, meeting the legal and ethical requirements that exist
in regards to the freedom of information, especially in respect to an individual's right to know the basis on which action affecting his/her career may be taken. Those involved
in the process must have a strong professional concern for
the individual's right of privacy; information to which they
may have access, and actions that they may be asked to take,
should be treated as confidential matters. While it may be

difficult to approach an honest evaluation of one's peers with the knowledge that what one has to say will be seen by the individual, it is important to recognize that the individual must have the ability to see what is being used in evaluating his/her performance, especially if questions or problems arise. Professional librarians should feel comfortable with attempting to make honest, objective evaluations of a colleague's performance without worrying about those evaluations being seen by the individual who is being evaluated. In particular the problems of maintaining good working relationships, and even friendships, should be minimized if the evaluation is based, as has been suggested, upon well-developed job descriptions and well-defined goals and objectives. It may help to stress that those who are providing evaluations are being asked only to evaluate those aspects of a person's performance with which they have direct contact, and are not being asked to make a recommendation for or against a specific action such as promotion. The actual recommendations for such actions may be made by an advisory committee to the Director, and may be based on peer evaluations received, but such recommendations, which must also be made available to the individual, can be a summary of evaluations received and should seek to attain a balance of positive and negative aspects in evaluating the person's overall performance. As has been indicated, it is most essential that, whatever the process, the information received and the basis for the recommendations not become a subject of widespread discussion and gossip within the library.

A further point to consider is the relationship of evaluation procedures to, and use of the criteria in, the hiring process. This is frequently overlooked, with the result that new library faculty may be hired without being adequately informed of the criteria and may suddenly find out about them shortly before the evaluation process begins. This puts new faculty at a severe disadvantage. It is necessary to include discussion of evaluation procedures and criteria as part of the hiring process. An open discussion with each applicant on this topic should result in the hiring of faculty who was more prepared and qualified to meet the criteria for evaluation from the first day on the job. It is also critical that the criteria be used as a basis for determining the level of appointment for new staff so that difficulties do not arise later because an individual was appointed at a rank inappropriate to his/her background and experience.

Advantages and Problems

One of the greatest advantages of a peer review process in an academic library is the impetus that it may provide to the development of stated criteria, clear job descriptions for each faculty member, and a system of performance evaluation based on goals and objectives. The formalization of the process in those respects allows the librarian to more readily understand where he/she stands in regard to reappointment, promotion and tenure, and to have a firm basis for discussing those matters with his/her supervisor. At the same time the supervisor can more easily see areas of strength and point out those areas that need improvement.

Peer review also enhances the librarian's position within the library. It allows for staff participation in the decision-making process and assumes shared responsibility for faculty development and personnel decisions. The growth potential of one's peers becomes everyone's concern. It enables the library faculty to look at the overall personnel picture and determine its strengths and weaknesses.

Perhaps the greatest problem is that early attempts at peer evaluation may be hindered by lack of sophistication and expertise in the process. It can take several rounds of evaluations before everyone feels comfortable with and understands the process more fully. During that time the process is likely to require some refinement and modification. It is essential not to develop an expectation that the entire process will work perfectly the first time around. It is also important to realize that the process cannot be one that is borrowed from another library or based solely on national standards. Any such process must be adapted to the political realities of the individual library and institution.

Peer evaluation for the faculty may also cause some dissension among the rest of the library staff, who often are not given the opportunity for input. This can be especially difficult when a library faculty member supervises and works closely only with support staff, but is then evaluated by the rest of the faculty. Where appropriate, opportunities for input from non-faculty staff members should be allowed.

Responsibilities

With the establishment of a peer evaluation process

come certain responsibilities for all who are involved. The
library administration must see that adequate job descriptions
and a method of performance evaluation are developed. The
evaluation process must be explained clearly to all persons
involved prior to the time evaluations are done, so that mis-
understandings do not occur. The information gleaned during
the evaluation process must be fairly assessed and applied
consistently to all faculty members. Lastly, the library administrator must provide a fair evaluation for each faculty
member and be willing to discuss that evaluation with each
one in an open manner.

      The library faculty involved in the evaluation process
must apply the criteria fairly and consistently to all. The
appropriate confidentiality of information must be maintained.
Discussion of personality traits and personality conflicts
should be avoided unless these traits are clearly detrimental
to an individual's job performance. Lastly, the library faculty must seek to provide honest and objective evaluations
and not be swayed by personal likes or dislikes, nor by the
hope that a favorable evaluation of another will bring a favorable evaluation in return.

      Finally, the individual being evaluated must provide
peers and administrators with sufficient and clearly presented
data upon which a realistic evaluation can be based. While
it is easier said than done, the individual must also be prepared to accept the evaluation and judgment of peers. This
should provide a balance of negative and positive aspects of
the individual's performance, and the negative comments should
be accepted and used as a basis for improving future performance. Positive comments should not give the individual a
sense of complacency.

Conclusion

      The peer evaluation process, as one writer recently
put it, is "an idea whose time continues to come."[7] It is up
to us to develop criteria that reflect our special skills and
expertise and at the same time allow for our professional
growth and development as faculty members and as academic
librarians.

Notes

1. Faculty Status for Academic Librarians: A History and
   Policy Statements. Chicago: American Library Association, 1975.

2. McAnally, Arthur M. "Privileges and Obligations of
   Academic Status," in Branscomb, Lewis C., ed., The
   Case for Faculty Status for Academic Librarians. Chi-
   cago: American Library Association, 1970, p. 4-8.

3. Hayashikawa, Doris. "Library Faculty Evaluation: The
   Texas A&M Case," Texas Library Journal 51:68-71, 1975.

4. Ibid.

5. Yeh, Thomas Yen-Ran. "Library Peer Evaluation for
   Promotion and Merit Increase: How It Works," College
   and Research Libraries 34:270-4, July, 1973.

6. Person, Roland. "Library Faculty Evaluation: An Idea
   Whose Time Continues to Come," Journal of Academic
   Librarianship 5:142-7, July, 1979.

7. Ibid.

THE SHARING OF LIBRARY PERSONNEL

by Norman D. Stevens

Abstract

At a time when libraries are seeking to find new ways of cooperating, inadequate attention has been given to the sharing of personnel. This essay explores the background, history, and theory of various aspects of the cooperative use of personnel. Attention is given to the types of services that can be provided on a cooperative basis, ways in which such services can best be provided, the benefits to individual librarians as well as to libraries, potential barriers to the establishment of effective programs of personnel sharing, and problems that can arise in implementing these programs.

Introduction

It has become almost trite to say that American libraries are now undergoing a period of change which, in both its magnitude and rate, is unlike any that has faced them in the past. Budgetary constraints are becoming more significant and permanent. Serious questions are being raised about time-honored collection development and selection policies and practices. Automation, at both the local and the network level, is becoming more widespread. The basic organizational patterns of libraries continue to change, especially in response to changes in the expectations and role of staff. A wide range of other developments and demands, many of them arising from outside the library, are leading toward much more meaningful cooperative efforts.

Most cooperative efforts to date have concentrated on cataloging and processing, the sharing of library resources, or, recently, the sharing of automated activities relating to the joint use of large bibliographic data bases. Many of these programs have been effective and have enabled the participating

libraries to provide a wider range of materials to their users
and to improve the depth, quality, and speed of their services. Such cooperative programs have, of course, often
had an impact on the personnel needs and on the utilization
of personnel in the participating libraries. For the most
part, however, such programs have not been designed with
those needs in mind and, as a result, have had only limited,
and almost incidental, impact in that regard.

Since historically libraries have dealt with books and
the information in them, it is natural that cooperation has
focused mainly on how to make material owned by one library
more readily available to the users of another library. Much
of the recent concern with the sharing of resources, though,
has risen from a situation in which personnel costs have come
to occupy an increasingly larger share of library budgets.
Libraries long ago should have more seriously addressed the
question of what can be done to reduce, or stabilize, that
portion of the budget devoted to personnel, in order, among
other things, to help preserve acquisitions funds and collection
growth. It is now imperative to do so. In the typical large
academic library more than 70% of the operating budget may
be spent on personnel and less than 30% on collections. Inflation is driving up the cost of library materials so that the
same dollars buy substantially less. At the same time, however, it is driving up the salary and wages portion of the
budget. In these circumstances attention must be paid to the
personnel aspect of the budget and, in particular, to ways in
which, through cooperative efforts and other means, better use
can be made of staff.

As new services become available, as the management
of libraries becomes more complex, and as demands from
users become more and more sophisticated, there is a steady
demand for substantial improvement in the quality of library
service. This is accompanied by a demand for specialized
staff, which is both expensive and in short supply, to help
libraries meet these needs. Even the largest individual libraries cannot provide the specialized staff or the quality of
service required with the resources available to them. The
cooperative use of personnel is becoming an essential element
of good library service.

In an earlier essay, "Beyond the Promises of Automation, "[1] I considered the effects that automation would have on
American academic libraries. I suggested that, in a number
of respects, automation was likely to encourage or allow li-

braries to make more effective use of staff, especially through programs designed to share personnel. In this essay, after reviewing the history of personnel sharing programs in libraries, I intend to discuss various aspects of the sharing of personnel. I also plan to address such issues as the ways in which such sharing can best be accomplished, the advantages of such programs, the benefits to individual librarians and libraries, possible barriers, and the problems that can arise.

History

Most programs of library cooperation that have been developed in America have, in fact, contained some element of personnel sharing even though that has not been the primary emphasis of the program. Because this is a different way of looking at cooperative programs, it seems appropriate to review a few past and present cooperative library programs from that perspective. This history section is an attempt to describe some of the kinds of programs that have existed, or are now in operation, which involve the sharing of personnel. It is intended, in that respect, to set a framework for the discussion that follows.

The activity that has had the longest history of using personnel cooperatively in American libraries has been in cataloging. For well over 100 years, various cooperative programs to share cataloging copy have been suggested and tried. These have all been based on the concept that original cataloging is a demanding and time-consuming professional effort requiring a high level of intellectual skill. Once that intellectual work has been performed for a book in one library by one cataloger, other libraries should then be able to save personnel costs by making use of that same product. This was the concept behind Jewett's ill-fated proposal to use stereotype plates for cataloging copy in 1853. The Library of Congress's program for the sale of cataloging cards, which began in 1901, was also based on the ability of other libraries to share the services of the specialized cataloging staff at the Library of Congress. That kind of service was later expanded through the National Union Catalog (although its primary emphasis was on the location and sharing of resources), by the cooperative cataloging program in its various forms, by the development of the MARC format and the distribution of MARC tapes, by various aspects of NPAC (National Program for Acquisitions and Cataloging) and, ultimately, by the development, and subsequent expansion, of on-line cataloging systems and services as offered by OCLC and others.

Out of those activities, and especially out of the growth
and expansion of OCLC, came the development, in the late
1960s and early 1970s, of what has become one of the most
successful broad-scale library cooperative programs: the establishment and development of state and multi-state library
networks. These networks, which now encompass a substantial portion of the country, exist primarily to facilitate the
sharing of large bibliographic data bases, and thus cataloging
copy, through the use of national services. In doing so they
facilitate the sharing of cataloging personnel. On an overall
basis the use of these networks, and through them of cooperative cataloging, has already had an impact in reducing the
number and the use of professional catalogers in American
libraries. These networks are also predicated upon the development of a central office staffed by personnel who are
funded by a number of libraries and who exist to provide
those libraries with specialized services, such as training in
the use of automated cataloging services.

Likewise, over the past decade a steadily increasing
number of local consortia have come into existence. These
consortia are based on the concept that a group of libraries
in an immediate geographic area can achieve economies through
the sharing of resources. These consortia are usually most
effective when they involve the joint hiring of a central staff
which can plan and carry out certain activities, such as production of union lists, that are essential to the sharing of resources but which cannot effectively be carried out on a vol-
unteer basis.

Preceding the development of networks and consortia
there were a substantial number of cases, well documented
in the literature, in which a group of libraries joined to develop processing centers designed to centralize all technical
processing activities for those libraries. Such centers employ a large number of staff, hired on a cooperative basis,
to handle a large volume of work on a more efficient basis
than the libraries could accomplish individually.

Some academic libraries--for the most part
larger research libraries--have on occasion shared
staff members with special competencies for which
there is inadequate need in a single library. Area
or language experts such as Burmese catalogers,
or subject specialist librarians such as paleographers
or papyrologists have served multiple institutions.
Formats for these arrangements have varied. In

some cases, one institution has employed the specialist and sold his services to another; in other
cases, joint appointments have been used; sometimes
consortial appointments have served the purpose. ...
Where such expertise is very seldom needed, of
course, libraries have tended to purchase it in the
ad hoc consulting market instead of on a continuing
retainer basis. [2]

Three specific institutional arrangements are most
commonly cited as examples of how the largest saving in library costs, including personnel costs, can be achieved through
the merger of library services for two or more academic institutions in the same geographic area. In each of these
cases, while the institutions have retained their identity, they
have combined to operate one joint library. All were established during the 1930s, when financial resources were scarce,
and all involve private institutions which received financial
support from private foundations to assist in the establishment
of the joint service.

In California the Honnold Library provides centralized
service for the Claremont Graduate School as well as for the
Claremont Men's, Harvey Mudd, Pitzer, Pomona, and Scripps
Colleges. Services are centralized through that Library, but
there are also separate college libraries at two of the institutions. In Atlanta the Atlanta University Center serves Atlanta University, and Clark, Morehouse, Morris Brown, and
Spelman Colleges, and the Interdenominational Theological
Center, all of which are located on contiguous campuses. In
1932 Atlanta University constructed a central library, within
the University Center, designed to serve all of those institutions, each of which still maintains its own separate library.
Finally the Joint University Libraries of Nashville were established in 1936 by Vanderbilt University, George Peabody College, and Scarrit College, all of which are continguous. The
Joint University Libraries administer a general central library
as well as specialized libraries in education, law, medicine,
and music. In this case the merger has been complete and
separate institutional libraries are not maintained. [3] As David
Kaser, for a number of years Director of the Joint University
Libraries, indicates:

Their experience seems to permit some generalizations. They become cost beneficial only when
one central library can result in the elimination of
two or more other libraries, a situation which can

probably obtain only when the central library is within walking distance of all. Total merger can under
such circumstances result in minimal duplication
and maximal economies of scale. There are some
counterbalancing costs to the participating institutions in that they must foresake autonomous library
decision-making and thereafter resort to political
processes to gain desired ends. Also, as in any
troika, the organization can advance only as fast
as its slowest horse. As the fiscal fortunes of the
participants wax and wane unsynchronously, the
joint library will receive only that level of support
thought by the waning member to be for the moment
fundable. It seems clear that under the best of
circumstances merged libraries will succeed financially, but without such circumstances they have
little to offer. [4]

For many years these remained the primary examples
of merged library services designed to provide one set of
services and staff for several institutions. They were viewed,
for the most part, as isolated examples of a particular kind
of library development suitable for peculiar times and circumstances, and they were not duplicated elsewhere. The
return of the same kind of financial constraints that existed
in the 1930s, together with a new phenomenon, has brought
about the revival of the concept of joint library service in
the past several years. The new phenomenon is the existence
in one geographic area of several state-supported institutions
of higher education. This has brought about the development
of the concept of a single campus, with certain basic services
including the library operated jointly, even though the institutions may retain their own identity.

In Denver, for example, the bringing together on one
campus of the University of Colorado at Denver, Metropolitan
State College, and the Community College of Denver has resulted in the merger of three libraries, including their staffs,
into the Auraria Libraries administered by the University of
Colorado at Denver. [5] Still partially in the planning stage,
although some construction has been completed, is a similar
venture in Waterbury, Connecticut. There development is
under way for a single campus to serve the Mattatuck Community College, a two-year branch of the University of Connecticut at Waterbury, and the Waterbury State Technical College.
That development will eventually bring with it a central library
designed to serve all three institutions. [6]

In these cases both the geographic proximity of the institutions on a single campus and their relationship to a common funding source should augur well for their ultimate success, since some of the problems cited by Kaser, especially
the inequality in funding levels, should be avoided. It is likely, despite a general decline in the building of new campuses
and new buildings by state-supported institutions of higher education, that this model will have great appeal. Other examples
of this kind of cooperation in the merger of library services
and the joint use of personnel, whether by choice or by govern-
mental mandates, are likely to occur over the next decade.

Institutional rivalry, even within similar systems, is
likely to be the chief obstacle to this approach to cooperation.
That was demonstrated in a slightly different experiment, also
involving state-supported institutions, which took place in
southern West Virginia in the early 1970s. Bluefield State
College and Concord College, located about 19 miles apart,
had been in existence for some time. In the experiment a
single President directed their activities under an arrangement that merged those two schools administratively with the
newly created Southern West Virginia College of Graduate
Studies, which had no separate library. Other administrative
staff, including the Director of Libraries and Media Services,
also served the three institutions. The Director of Libraries and
Media Services was responsible for the joint administration of the
staff of the two libraries and spent time at each location. The
other major sharing of personnel in the libraries occurred in a
reclassification project in which a special project staff worked
first at one library and subsequently at the other to reclassify
the collections from Dewey to LC. The combined administration of the libraries worked reasonably well. After about
three years, however, the pressures for local autonomy ultimately led the institutions to return to their independent status.
That brought with it an end to the administrative merger of
the libraries. 7

A similar, but more successful, example of the administrative consolidation of two academic libraries has occurred
with two private liberal arts colleges in eastern Pennsylvania.
In 1973 Cedar Crest College and Muhlenberg College, located
about a mile apart in Allentown, elected to explore ways in
which they could work more effectively to improve their relationships without merging and losing their separate identities.
The fortuitous circumstance of the retirement of the Librarian
at Muhlenberg led to a decision to hire a director with administrative responsibility for both libraries. Since then the
two libraries have functioned under a single director. Under

that arrangement they have worked to combine all technical
services in one location, to utilize a single membership in
PALINET to use OCLC services, and, more recently, to develop a combined public services staff responsible for providing coverage at the reference desks as well as for providing
bibliographic instruction at both institutions. The larger base
of operations has enabled the libraries to hire reference staff
with more subject specialization and to make that specialization available to the users of both libraries. At present,
several members of the staff have joint appointments and the
possibility of combining both staffs into one unit administratively, through the use of such appointments, is being discussed. The major problem appears to have been in developing good working relationships between the staffs in a situation
where there had been some institutional rivalry. Nevertheless,
on the whole, this has proven to be an effective demonstration
of how libraries can work together in the sharing of personnel
resources. [8]

        In 1974 the Illinois State Library developed a program
of shared staffing for public libraries designed "to improve
the quality of library service in communities now unable to
afford professional staff; to assist libraries in the process of
meeting minimum standards by offering incentive through special personnel grants; and to establish a basis for co-operative
effort with long-range potential for developing larger units of
library service. "[9]   Through this program a professional librarian was assigned to cover two or three small local libraries in the same area.   This was done in six locations
throughout the state through three-year grants.   Initially the
librarians served on a larger library system staff and payroll
for two years, while providing combined services, but were
assigned directly to the two or three libraries at the end of
the second year, and remained on grant support for a final
year.   Although the program was initially envisioned as enabling libraries to hire a professional chief librarian, subsequent grants have been made to libraries that wish to share
positions in reference and information services, children's
programs, and services to the home-bound and the hearing-
impaired. [10]

        A number of other examples of specific sharing of
personnel among libraries, especially academic libraries,
have occurred in recent years and appear to be occurring
more and more frequently.   In some cases several libraries
combine to employ a staff member at another library to provide services for them.   In the CTUW Project in Connecticut,

for example, the libraries of Connecticut College, Trinity
College, the University of Connecticut, and Wesleyan University have combined to fund staff located at the Yale University
Library to facilitate interlibrary loan access to materials
there. [11]

More often this kind of sharing involves specialized
staff at one library developing programs, especially ones that
require a high level of initial development work, and sharing
those programs with the libraries of other institutions. A
considerable amount of this kind of activity is beginning to
take place in the area of personnel. The 1977/1978 annual
report of the Staff Development Officer of the Yale University
Library, for example, cites four instances of such sharing,
including the exchange of trainers and participants with the
libraries at the University of Connecticut and Princeton University. It frequently involves other staff and programs as
well. "The Sangamon Valley Library Consortium in central
Illinois agreed upon such a project in the spring of 1977. . . .
It was decided that one of the best ways the libraries could
strengthen each other was to co-operate in a series of continuing education workshops for members' staff. Four were
planned for the 1977-78 year, two on the acquisition, organization, and housing of nonprint materials, one on basic reference techniques for paraprofessionals, and one on library
instruction. Different institutions assumed responsibility for
each topic in keeping with their expertise. "[12]

The Office of Management Studies (OMS) of the Association of Research Libraries (ARL) is yet another example
of the sharing of specialized personnel resources. A combination of grant funds and support from member libraries
has enabled the ARL to develop a highly specialized staff at
the OMS which has in turn developed programs designed to
work effectively with individual libraries. Through the Management Review and Analysis Project (MRAP), the Collection
Analysis Project (CAP), and the Academic Library Development Program (ALDP), the Office of Management Studies has
provided this kind of specialized assistance to 32 libraries
since 1972. Through the development of other self-study
modules, including a Small Library Planning Program, a
Services Development Program, and an Organizational Training and Staff Development Program, the OMS expects, over
the next several years, to extend its ability to allow libraries
to share in the use of its specialized personnel. As those
programs expand, the central OMS staff will not be in a position to work directly with a larger number of libraries in

providing guidance and direction in the application of those
self-study modules.   To expand that capability the OMS is
now developing an Academic Library Program (ALP).   In
that program the OMS plans to train approximately 100 staff
members from individual academic libraries throughout the
country to serve as consultants to other libraries which wish
to use one or more of the self-study packages offered by the
Office. 13

There are numerous other examples of cooperative
programs that make use of the sharing of personnel.   This
survey is not complete and is not intended to be exhaustive.
In fact, as this paper was being written and ideas and drafts
were shared with others, new examples were constantly identified.   Unfortunately, in many cases these examples are inadequately reported in the professional literature.   Perhaps
it is because those who are involved in such programs see
them as merely local efforts and do not understand the extent
to which they are part of an increasingly important overall
development.   Certainly broader reporting on these kinds of
cooperative programs, with an emphasis on the personnel
sharing aspects, would be useful.   In most cases there is
little to suggest that, to date, these kinds of programs have
been approached as techniques for the sharing of personnel.
Rather they have most often been approached in a more traditional fashion as a technique for expanding and extending library services.   There has been, therefore, almost no discussion in the literature of cooperative programs as a means
of personnel sharing and no evaluation of the effectiveness of
particular kinds of programs, or recommendations for how
such programs might best be developed.

The examples that have been described have been used
to provide a background for understanding the ideas and comments that are to follow.   Because of the lack of previous
discussion of this concept in the literature, those ideas and
comments are largely theoretical.   They are not based, in
any detail, on an analysis of the programs that have been
described above.

Conditions

Given the strong justification that exists, libraries must
continue to explore and develop other programs for the cooperative use of personnel.   This is most likely to occur where
such programs are seen as enabling libraries to help reduce

or stabilize personnel costs, to make better use of personnel, or to have available to them a depth and breadth of personnel support that would not otherwise be possible.

For some time most of these programs will continue to be developed in response to local initiatives and opportunities and will continue to be seen primarily as a means of sharing services or programs rather than personnel. These programs are likely to develop primarily as the need for them arises, and as librarians come together to take advantage of personal contacts, network or other organizational memberships, and other opportunities that exist. As these kinds of programs continue to develop and to emphasize the personnel aspects, it should become possible to better formulate the conditions and circumstances that contribute to the success of this approach. It is essential to begin to develop a more coordinated approach to the cooperative use of personnel.

A number of factors enter into the conditions under which programs for the joint use of personnel might be tried. The same factors are likely to have a great deal to do with the success or failure of those programs. Important, but intangible, factors such as geography, individual personalities and attitudes, past history, and external constraints or pressures play a major role. Unfortunately we do not yet know enough about how these factors work to be able to identify more precisely what they are and whether they augur success or failure. Geographic proximity, for example, which enables staff to move easily from one location to another without serious disruption of personal living conditions, is one factor that should contribute to the success of a program. Since a number of the other factors remain intangible a subjective judgment on the part of those involved as to how they will affect a program is all that can be hoped for. Successful participation in similar ventures is perhaps the one factor that is most likely to persuade libraries to attempt other programs. Through such participation a clearer understanding of the possibilities and benefits, as well as of the limitations and problems, of such programs is likely to be developed by library administrators and staffs. That understanding is, in the long run, probably the most critical factor in encouraging other ventures.

It would seem that personnel services can reasonably be considered to be made available on a shared basis when they are expensive, or when they involve a high level of in-

tellectual work that can be used by others, or when they involve the development of specialized skills that may be used
on an infrequent basis by one library alone, or when the
skills are in short supply, or when they may be needed for
a fixed period of time rather than indefinitely. There is a
real need to evaluate this kind of cooperative program carefully in terms of the financial benefits and not to enter into
such arrangements lightly, no matter what the incentives or
pressures may be. In particular there is a need to develop
an effective means for evaluating the success or failure of a
program over time. This can perhaps best be done in the
context of developing specific performance standards agreed
on in advance by all concerned. While in any cooperative
program there may be intangible benefits to the individuals
and even to the libraries that participate, even those should
be described. In any case, it is only if programs are defined
in a realistic way and can be measured in terms of the specific benefits that accrue to the participants, that they should
be defined as successful, should be continued, and should be
used as the basis for other activities or the model for other
programs.

Areas of Personnel Sharing

There are a large number of library functions that can
appropriately be considered as areas for exploring the cooperative use of personnel. The historical survey above, even
though incomplete, suggests a number of such activities and
services. The following section of this paper attempts to
expand on those and to describe some other areas where such
programs might be considered. Again, the listing is not intended to be comprehensive or definitive; it is designed only
to suggest some of the kinds of services that might be considered in developing cooperative programs.

(1) Administrative Services

In recent years the administrative functions of libraries have tended to expand beyond the director to include a
range of specialized functions in such areas as budgeting,
personnel, planning, and purchasing. All of these require
increasing, and often extremely detailed, familiarity with
specialized areas of knowledge, legal requirements, new
techniques, technology, and similar fields. Often these are
areas in which libraries and librarians have not traditionally

had any expertise. In many cases even the person specifically assigned in a library to handle one of those functions finds
it difficult to develop and maintain a comprehensive understanding of all aspects of the function. These activities often
result in the development of programs that, with a minimal
expenditure of additional time and effort, can be used by other
libraries. The development, for example, of a training program on interviewing skills by the personnel officer of one
library may require a considerable initial expenditure of time
and effort. Once developed, such a program is likely to be
used over a period of time within the particular library, and,
with a minimal amount of additional effort, that same program
can be adapted and used in other libraries. Other specialized
administrative services offer the same opportunities.

     As the example of Cedar Crest and Muhlenberg Col-
leges demonstrates, the assignment of one individual to handle
the administrative duties of two or more separate libraries
is clearly feasible. By pooling resources and assignments
in this way, it is possible for two or more smaller libraries
to attract a higher calibre of individual, both because of the
likely ability to pay a higher salary and because of the ability
to offer a more challenging job assignment than they might be
able to do individually. This kind of cooperative use of personnel is also likely to provide a setting and direction that
will enable other aspects of library services involving personnel to be considered on a cooperative basis.

(2) Technical Services

     In the technical services area the time-worn example
of cooperative use of personnel is, as I have indicated, the
sharing of original cataloging skills. This will continue for
many years to be one of the most important areas of staff
sharing. There are, however, other technical services areas
that lend themselves equally well to such sharing. Specialized collection development programs and the selection of materials is one such area. A subject specialist in an area
such as Latin America, for example, should be able to serve
several institutions, assuming that the programs at some of
the institutions are of a relatively modest size. Having, on
a continuing basis, fundamental knowledge about the scope of
the academic programs and the library interests of each institution, that person should be able to function effectively
for each by: helping to establish standing orders based on
well-developed profiles; doing individual selection of titles by

reading journal reviews, scanning catalogs and national bibliographies, etc. ; maintaining good relationships with dealers
in various countries; purchasing or otherwise acquiring materials on buying trips; and helping in the establishment of other
appropriate collection development policies and programs. By
having one person serve two or more libraries in this way,
it should also be possible to develop a stronger program for
the cooperative acquisition of materials, and to minimize the
duplication of specialized and expensive works.

The conservation and preservation of library materials
also lends itself to the cooperative use of personnel, both
because of the highly specialized level of skills required,
which are currently in short supply, and because, in many
cases, short-term advice and assistance is needed to set up
programs that others can maintain, or to deal with particular
problems or emergencies. In addition, some aspects of this
kind of activity involve the purchase and use of expensive
equipment that it is not necessary for every library to own
and whose use involves specialized skills.

(3) Public Services

The tradition in the public services area that effective
provision of service to users normally requires on-the-spot
availability of personnel is a barrier to the development of
cooperative programs for the use of personnel in this aspect
of library service. Fortunately there are now examples,
such as the merger of the reference staffs at Cedar Crest
and Muhlenberg Colleges, that demonstrate that such programs
are possible and can be effective. A skilled reference subject specialist can assist in the development of reference
collections, can provide basic training to other members of
reference staffs in the use of specialized tools, can offer instruction to users on the basic bibliographic approach to the
field, and can be available, either directly or indirectly, to
answer reference questions and to offer other individualized
aid in the use of materials in two or more libraries.

The provision of on-line bibliographic search services
requires the development of highly sophisticated skills, which
vary for the different data bases that are available on-line,
and the level of use in many libraries of a particular data
base may be low. Since skill and speed in the use of such
tools come with practice and directly affect both the quality
and the cost of the service, there is a considerable advantage

in developing the expertise that comes with continued use.
In a single library that may not be possible. The development of these basic skills by one library's staff, when continued use is likely to be sporadic, is an expensive, and often a poor, means of providing the service. Cooperative
programs whereby personnel serving several libraries are
trained and offer these services to users of all of the libraries seems to be a reasonable approach to overcoming the
problems that often exist at the local level.

While many libraries have instituted programs of bibliographic instruction of one kind or another, the quality varies
greatly and generally seems to be in need of improvement.
Often such programs are hampered in their development by
the lack of staff with the necessary training and/or skill in
teaching, by the lack of staff time to do the necessary preparation, and by the lack of continuing opportunities to teach
and thus make use of skills and preparation. While some of
the content of such instruction may be specific to a particular
institution, the emphasis is generally on skills and tools that
are not as specific. The development of an effective program
can be quite time-consuming and is likely to contain a number
of elements that lend themselves to repetitive use and to involve specialized skills that may not be widely used in one
library.

Finally there are a large number of other public service areas (e.g., the development of exhibits, programs,
publications, etc.) in which, in one way or another, the staff
involved in the planning and carrying out of such activities
could effectively serve two or more libraries.

(4) Other Areas

More and more libraries are engaged in activities and
programs that fall beyond the scope of the traditional breakdown of administrative, technical, or public services. Generally these activities are of a highly specialized nature and,
for that reason, should lend themselves to the sharing of
staff. Automation is one such activity. The emerging state
and multi-state library networks already provide many services involving the cooperative use of personnel in this area.
While their focus has largely been on training in the use of
on-line cataloging services, all of these networks, to one degree or another, now find themselves engaged in providing
their members with general automation consulting services.

In many cases the libraries have no specialized systems staff of their own and may not yet have other automated services. As those libraries consider other automated services, especially turnkey systems that may not require the employment of specialized in-house staff, they are likely to want and need expert advice and assistance from staff, other than that of potential vendors, with specialized skills. Even libraries with large-scale independent automation activities are likely to find that they too need advice and assistance, especially as they move into areas, such as telecommunications, that require highly specialized skills and knowledge that a local automation/systems staff may not have available and may not be able to develop readily. In the past various efforts have been made to transfer software systems developed at one library to another, in recognition of the sharing of specialized personnel skills that can take place. In some cases these efforts have worked well but often they have not because the programs required continued attention from somebody familiar with them after they had been transferred. More consideration should be given in this kind of exchange to the need to share not only programs but also the personnel responsible for their development. That personnel might assist in the initial implementation and adaptation and in the transfer and training of the staff responsible for the continued maintenance and operation of the system.

Libraries are also faced with the need to examine carefully a wide range of specialized problems (e.g., studies of organization, the provision of new services, the development of committee structures, etc.). Often this involves an extensive amount of planning and consideration and, through that planning and consideration, the development of specialized knowledge and skills. Traditionally this has been an area in which, either through a review of the literature or/through correspondence and conversation with colleagues at other libraries, librarians have sought in an informal way to share and make use of each other's expertise. Generally, however, that has been done on a limited and informal basis and there has not been, except perhaps in the area of building planning, any extensive use of shared personnel. As these activities become more extensive and more intensive the development of more structured and formal programs for the sharing of personnel and their skills would seem to be appropriate. The development, for example, among a group of libraries of some kind of skills bank, and the ability to utilize people and their skills in a relatively simple way, might be one possibility.

There seems to be little question, therefore, that it is
possible to identify a number of areas in which libraries can
and should move more effectively to develop programs for the
joint use of personnel. But how to do so and, perhaps equally important, how to weigh the advantages and disadvantages
of doing so and how to evaluate the success or failure of such
programs will require careful attention.

Structure and Organization

Just as the conditions under which cooperative programs
of personnel sharing might best succeed cannot be specified in
great detail, so it is difficult to describe precisely the kind
of structure under which such programs can best be provided.
Much, of course, depends on the type or kind of service being offered, the number of libraries involved, the relationship
of those libraries and their institutions to one another, the
scope and intended length of projects, and similar factors.
No one solution can fit all situations.

A number of models do exist, as has been demonstrated
in the historical survey above, and a careful review of those
models in considering and devising new programs is perhaps
the best approach that can be taken at the present time.
Again, it should be pointed out that, with some exceptions,
those models were not developed with personnel sharing as
the primary goal. The exceptions, such as the merged libraries, the sharing of a director by Cedar Crest and Muhlenberg, and the Illinois State Library program, offer perhaps
the best models to be examined. The establishment of demonstration projects specifically oriented to the sharing of personnel, with careful attention being paid to the structure of
those projects, and an evaluation of the structure, needs to
be explored.

The exchange or rotation of personnel from one library
to another is the simplest level of personnel sharing. What
are normally described as exchange programs, however, per-
tain largely to cases where individual librarians are seeking
to exchange jobs in order to improve their own skills and to
acquire a better understanding of their job. Under the kind
of circumstances being considered in this paper the emphasis
is on a quite different level of exchange. It is a level at
which the libraries involved are seeking, as part of their
regular program, to make use of personnel from other libraries on a formal basis to develop and strengthen that program.

Such exchanges are likely to be the most reasonable approach in dealing with libraries in close geographic proximity, in dealing with circumstances in which a packaged program developed and used at one library can be adapted for or presented at other libraries, and in ad hoc situations where informality and personal contacts may form the best basis for the development of a program.   They may also be the best approach in establishing programs initially, since the interaction that occurs can help build a relationship which will subsequently support other kinds of arrangements.   While, at least initially, a loose structure may be preferable, it is undoubtedly desirable, especially if the program is of any magnitude or is likely to last over a period of time, not to depend simply on good will and the exchange of correspondence.   Some kind of written memorandum of understanding, which clearly spells out the rights and responsibilities of the libraries involved, should be provided.

As programs grow in size and complexity, or take on a more permanent aspect (e. g. , the joint employment of a subject area specialist), a written memorandum of understanding may no longer be adequate.   Where additional personnel are to be hired by one library or another, or where substantial payments of money may be scheduled over a period of time, some kind of formal contractual agreement is required. In such cases those agreements must involve the parent institution, not just the libraries, in order to satisfy legal requirements and to be certain that all institutional requirements and obligations are fully satisfied.   This kind of arrangement is not to be undertaken lightly and should, therefore, be done only when there is a well developed and well defined program to which there is a firm commitment on the part of all involved.   In many cases such contractual agreements might best be undertaken only after a more informal, preliminary program has been tried.

If a number of libraries are involved, or if the program involves the hiring of new personnel for a service not available from an existing library, a third-party arrangement, such as the use of a local consortium or a state or multistate network, may offer certain advantages.   This approach may also be desirable as programs become larger and more complex, and as they involve highly specialized personnel (e. g. , conservation specialists) who may require specialized settings and equipment.   The provision of such services through a consortium or network may also allow for a more

lasting and a more equitable basis for arrangements to be
made.   Through the use of a third-party arrangement more
precise techniques for budgeting and for maintaining equity
may be developed.

Advantages and Benefits

Programs of this kind are not likely to be undertaken
unless it is clear that there are certain advantages and benefits to the participating libraries.   In part those advantages
and benefits have been described as other aspects have been
discussed above.   There are, however, other aspects of such
programs that may be of particular benefit to the libraries involved and to the personnel involved, as well as to some degree to the profession at large.

For the library that makes use of personnel there is
the clear-cut advantage of benefiting from a level of skill and
expertise that might not otherwise be available in dealing with
particular matters.   In addition there are likely to be a series
of intangible benefits.   Among those are the contact that it
provides for staff with other professional personnel and with
new ideas and approaches to problems.   Above all, such programs must provide a clear-cut financial benefit to the participating library or, at least, make available to it a service
that it would not otherwise have.

The contact that it provides with other professional
personnel must also be viewed as having a distinct advantage
for the individual librarian, by providing a much broader perspective of the library, of individual jobs, and of the profession.   Both for the participating librarian and for those who
are otherwise involved in such programs, these kinds of personnel sharing programs can be important developmental tools.

Problems and Barriers

No matter how essential a cooperative program involving the sharing of personnel seems to be, no matter how
carefully the arrangements for such a program may be worked
out, and no matter what the cost benefits may be, there are
a considerable number of problems and barriers that may be
encountered.   While some of these (e.g., effective performance)
may be no different from the problems encountered by an

individual library in dealing with its own personnel, a cooperative arrangement may make those problems more difficult to deal with.   In addition there are a number of problems that are unique to a cooperative program and that, unless effectively considered in advance, may create serious difficulties. These problems may be characterized as ones of quality of service, equity, local autonomy, loyalty, and staff attitudes.

One area of major concern in developing programs for the cooperative use of personnel should be with the quality of service.   By delegating to others, over whom there may be only limited control, responsibility for the provision of services for which the library ultimately will be held accountable, a library exposes itself to considerable potential difficulty.   This is perhaps especially true for academic libraries, and most especially true for those academic libraries that have a strong history and tradition of faculty control.   Except for the most basic programs, simple faith and trust are not adequate.   There must be, for the sake of all parties involved, performance standards established in advance and used as a means of measuring the quality of the service provided.   In addition there must be control mechanisms that allow the libraries involved to exercise some continuing influence over the development and provision of services.   It is for that reason that it is vitally important in the development of governance structures for consortia or networks to allow each library to participate, or to have a reasonable chance to participate, directly in the policy-making and control of the consortium or network.

A second major concern is equity.   How can a library be certain that it is getting the service it bargained for and that it is paying only its fair share of the costs?   Performance standards and a method of evaluation are again important.   In the long run, of course, it may well be a subjective impression, not a precise measure, that governs a library's decision as to whether or not any program is meeting its needs at a reasonable cost.   In programs involving the cooperative use of personnel, the development of an agreed-upon method of payment that all parties accept as reasonable, and a mechanism that allows all of the parties to participate in periodically reviewing the costs and the charging mechanisms and structure is essential.

A third concern is the question of local autonomy. Programs involving the sharing of personnel are likely to lead inevitably to some degree of standardization and, in fact, are likely to increase in effectiveness as standardization is achieved. On the other hand, local control and autonomy in the development and content of programs may be reviewed as essential by some libraries. The conflict between local needs, whether real or perceived, and standardization may lead to increasing problems in programs of personnel sharing. These problems may be insoluble unless some larger entity, such as a parent institution, intervenes and provides the necessary leadership and direction, or unless a strong consortium or network that can balance those needs and can provide direction exists or is established.

Related to that concern is the potential for creating a situation in which the individuals have divided loyalty and may find it difficult to maintain a balance in their work. A subject specialist bibliographer employed by one library but providing services for another may find it difficult in recommending a rare or unusual item for purchase, to suggest that it be bought by the second library, even though it may more appropriately belong there. It is only, however, through the development of an adequate understanding of the program and of a strong professional sense of responsibility that such problems can be overcome.

In other respects as well, staff attitudes and perceptions may be a significant problem. The success or failure of programs involving the joint use of personnel is likely to depend as much upon such intangible matters as on the quality and benefits of the program. This may be most true where programs involve a smaller number of libraries in an immediate geographic area, since the staff of the libraries involved are likely to already have firmly developed perceptions of, and attitudes towards, one another that cannot be easily changed. This kind of problem may also be exaggerated in situations in which the library staffs, whether rightly or wrongly, view such cooperative efforts in the sharing of personnel as threats to local levels of employment and job security. Finally, how performance standards for individual staff are developed and how their performance is ultimately measured, when two or more supervisors who may have differing expectations are involved, can create problems in this respect unless there is careful planning in advance.

Undoubtedly other problems exist and certainly in developing any kind of new program unforeseen difficulties often arise. In general it appears that problems can be minimized to the extent that formalized programs with well established

guidelines are established. Certainly, too, in programs that
involve the sharing of personnel a degree of flexibility and
understanding on the part of those involved is required. Expectations may be high and guidelines should be met, but the
ability to respond to new circumstances and to adapt programs
as required is also essential.

Conclusion

While there are an increasing number of library programs that are built around the cooperative use of personnel,
there is a strong justification for even more extensive development of such programs. While such programs may present
a series of problems and difficulties, it seems clear that
those difficulties can be overcome by careful planning and
structuring.

It is essential for all libraries to make the most effective use of all of their resources. There are imaginative
ways in which libraries, by working together, can begin to
share staff on a continuing basis. By doing so libraries
should be able not only to maintain existing levels of service
but should be able to begin to offer their users a higher
quality of specialized services based on access to more highly qualified staff.

It will not be a simple matter to develop such programs. Fundamental institutional decisions relating to the
reallocation of resources away from the local level will have
to be made. Such decisions are not made easily and cannot
be made without well developed programs that provide for the
necessary safeguards and controls. Library staffs will require substantial reorientation and will need to acquire a
stronger sense of professional loyalty. They will have to be
shown, as will others, that the development of such programs
can improve the quality and range of services, and can provide for reasonable transition in whatever impact there is on
local operations, including levels of personnel.

Resource sharing, whether of collections or personnel,
is not the ultimate answer to all library problems. It is only
one approach. There is, and will continue to be, a strong
need for local collections, personnel, and services. Libraries are, after all, primarily designed to provide materials
and services directly to users. Resource sharing, in whatever form, has limits. We have not yet, however, begun

seriously to explore the sharing of library personnel to provide for services on a cooperative basis.

Notes

1. Norman D. Stevens. "Beyond the Promises of Automa-
    tion, " in Essays for Ralph Shaw. Metuchen, N. J. :
    Scarecrow Press, 1975, p. 190-206.

2. David Kaser and Jinnie Y. Davis. The Viability of
    Merging Three Academic Libraries in Worcester. New
    York: Carnegie Corporation, 1977, p. 22-3.

3. The best discussion of such joint libraries is to be found
    in Richard D. Johnson, "Joint Academic Libraries, " in
    Advances in Librarianship. N. Y. : Academic Press,
    1975, p. 322-54.

4. Kaser, op. cit. , p. 31.

5. Telephone and written communications with Donald E.
    Riggs, Director of Auraria Libraries.

6. Personal knowledge.

7. Telephone and written communications with Donald E.
    Riggs, formerly Director of Libraries & Media Services
    for those institutions.

8. Telephone communication with Patricia Sacks, Director
    of Libraries for Cedar Crest and Muhlenberg Colleges.

9. Illinois Libraries 58:603, 1976.

10. Illinois Nodes, September, 1978, p. 5.

11. Personal knowledge.

12. C&RL News # 7:190, 1978.

13. There is a variety of information available about the
    OMS. The most readily available current information
    is to be found in the Association of Research Libraries
    Minutes.

BIBLIOGRAPHY OF WRITINGS FROM THE SEMINAR

BRUNTJEN, SCOTT.
"Librarians in a Time of Uncertainty," The Journal of Academic Librarianship 4:158-9, 1978.

Source Documents for American Bibliography: Three "McMurtrie Manuals." Halifax, Nova Scotia: Dalhousie University, 1978. (Dalhousie University Libraries and Dalhousie University School of Library Service. Occasional Paper 18).

Douglas McMurtrie: Bibliographer and Historian of Printing. Metuchen, N.J.: Scarecrow Press, 1979 (with Melissa Young).

BURNS, ELISABETH S.
"The United States Nondepository Library: A Commendation," The Journal of Academic Librarianship 3:286-7, 1977.

DANIELS, WES.
"How to Hire a Library Director: The Erewhon Experience," The Journal of Academic Librarianship 3:211-2, 1977.

"An Alternative to Library School," Library Journal 103:1702-3, 1978.

GUNNING, KATHLEEN.
"Increasing the Reference Librarians Participation in the Research Process," The Journal of Academic Librarianship 4:216-7, 1978.

HILL, BONNIE NAIFEH.
"Collection Development: The Right and Responsibility of Librarians," The Journal of Academic Librarianship 3:285-6, 1977.

KIJANKA, DOROTHY.
"Faculty Library Privileges, " The Journal of Academic
Librarianship 4:28-9, 1978.

LINDGREN, SUSAN L.
"The Academic Library in a Schooled Society, " The
Journal of Academic Librarianship 3:212-3, 1977.

LITTLEFIELD, KAREN A.
"In Search of a Panacea, " The Journal of Academic Librarianship 3:342-3, 1978.

MATHEWS, WILLIAM D.
"A Siege of Committees, " The Journal of Academic Librarianship 4:378, 1978.

SHERBY, LOUISE S.
"Academic Librarian: Librarian or Faculty Member?"
The Journal of Academic Librarianship 4:379-80, 1978.

STEVENS, NORMAN D.
"Keeper of the Library Past, " Wilson Library Bulletin
51:841-3, 1977.

"Modernizing OCLC's Governance, " Library Journal
102:2216-9, 1977.

Review of William H. Kurth and David S. Zubatsky,
Recommended Procedures for the Internal Financial Auditing
of University Libraries, in The Journal of Academic Librarianship 4:34-5, 1978.

"An Innovative Approach to Collection Management, "
Collection Management 2:25-8, 1978.

"An Observation on Shelving Practice, " Library Journal
103:1236, 1978.

"A Hard Look at Reserve, " The Journal of Academic
Librarianship 4:86-7, 1978.

Review of Jamie J. Levine and Timothy Logan, On-Line
Resource Sharing, in Library Journal 103:1238, 1978.

Review of On-Line Information Retrieval Systems, in Library Journal 103:1576, 1978.

Review of Patricia Senn Breivik, Open Admissions and the Academic Library, in Library Quarterly 48:345-7, 1978.

"The Writings of Paul S. Dunkin: A Review Article," Library Resources and Technical Services 22:349-60, 1978.

"Writing for Publication," Collection Management 3:21-9, 1979.

WHO WE ARE

SCOTT BRUNTJEN

Scott Bruntjen is now Executive Director of the Pittsburgh Regional Library Center (PRLC). At the time the Seminar began he was Associate Professor and Head of Public Services at the Shippensburg (Pa.) State College Library. He previously held positions at the State Library of Massachusetts and the Seven Rivers Library Cooperative in Iowa. Mr. Bruntjen received his master's in library science from the University of Iowa, and a master's in political science and a doctorate in library administration from Simmons College. With Carol Rinderknecht he is joint editor of the Checklist of American Imprints for the period from 1831 on. He reviews for Choice, College & Research Libraries, and RQ.

ELISABETH S. BURNS

Elisabeth S. Burns is Serials Librarian and Interlibrary Loan Librarian at the Roger Williams College Library. She received her bachelor's degree from Vassar College and her master's in library science from the University of Rhode Island. Mrs. Burns participated in developing and teaching, with the other librarians at Roger Williams College, a three-credit course in Library Research Methods for undergraduates which was first offered in 1977.

WES DANIELS

Wes Daniels is currently a student in the Harvard Law School and a Reference Librarian at the Harvard University Law Library. At the time the Seminar began he was Head of Technical Services at the University of Lowell Library where he had previously served as Periodicals Librarian. He received his bachelor's degree from Fordham University and his master's in library science from Simmons College

while working as a Harvard University Library Intern in the
Graduate School of Education Library. Mr. Daniels has been
a member of the Editorial Committee of the psychology journal State and Mind, an indexer for the Alternative Press Index, and a contributor of reviews to Library Journal.

KATHLEEN GUNNING

        Kathleen Gunning is Head of the Reference Department
at the Brown University Library. She received her bachelor's
degree from Brown University and her master's in library
science from the University of Rhode Island. She previously
served as Interlibrary Loan Librarian and as a Reference
Librarian at the Brown University Library. Miss Gunning
co-founded and co-edited the Brown Library News and edited
the Brown University Library's collection development policy
statement.

BONNIE NAIFEH HILL

        Bonnie Naifeh Hill is currently Assistant Head of the
Acquisitions Department and Selection Librarian at the Boston
University Library. She received her master's in library
science from the University of Oklahoma. She previously
served as Head of the Technical Services Division at the
Brookline Public Library and as Assistant Head of the Acquisitions Department and Serials Order Librarian at the
Boston University Library. Ms. Hill has been a book review-
er for Library Journal for several years and has also done
reviews for What's New in Scholarly Books and the Small
Press Review.

DOROTHY KIJANKA

        Dorothy Kijanka is Assistant University Librarian and
Head of Reader Services at the Fairfield University Library.
She received her bachelor's degree from the University of
Illinois and her master's in library service from Rutgers
University. She previously served as a Reference Librarian
at the Greenwich Public Library and at the Fairfield Univer-
sity Library. Mrs. Kijanka was a member of the Board of
Trustees and President of the Library Group of Southwestern
Connecticut in 1977/1978.

SUSAN L. LINDGREN

Susan L. Lindgren was a Reference Librarian at the
University of Vermont Library at the time the Seminar began.
She received her bachelor's degree from the University of
New Hampshire and her master's in library science from
the University of Michigan. During the course of the Seminar
Miss Lindgren moved to the University of Arizona to work on
a master's degree in business administration and was unable
to continue to participate in the Seminar after that point.

KAREN A. LITTLEFIELD

Karen A. Littlefield is currently a Children's Librarian
at the University of New Hampshire Library. At the time the
Seminar began she was a Cataloger and Coordinator of the
Catalog Department at the University of New Hampshire Library. Miss Littlefield received her bachelor's degree from
the University of New Hampshire and her master's degree
in library science from Simmons College.

WILLIAM D. MATHEWS

William D. Mathews was Director of the Systems Division at NELINET at the time the Seminar began. Subsequently he became Staff Associate for Information Technology with
the National Commission on Libraries and Information Science
before becoming Director of Planning and Development at The
Jockey Club in 1979. Prior to his service at NELINET he
served as Associate Director of Project TIP at the Massachusetts Institute of Technology Libraries. Mr. Mathews also
served as editor of the Journal of Library Automation.

LOUISE S. SHERBY

Louise S. Sherby is Head Reference Librarian at the
Rhode Island College Library. She received her bachelor's
degree from Hofstra University and her master's in librarianship from the University of Denver. She is currently working
on her doctorate in library science at Columbia University.
Miss Sherby previously served as a Reference Librarian in
both the Information Center and the History and Travel Departments of the Chicago Public Library.

NORMAN D. STEVENS

     Norman D. Stevens is currently University Librarian
at the University of Connecticut Library. He received his
bachelor's degree from the University of New Hampshire,
and his master's and doctorate in library service from Rutgers University. He previously served in a variety of capa-
cities at the University Library and the Graduate School of
Library Service at Rutgers University and as Acting Director
of University Libraries at the Howard University Library.
Mr. Stevens is the author of a number of articles, books,
miscellaneous contributions, and reviews. He was the originator of the Seminar and served as its Director.

APPENDIX

Proposal and Reports

to the

Council on Library Resources

PROPOSAL TO THE COUNCIL ON LIBRARY RESOURCES

There is general agreement that there exists a real need for an improvement in the quality of professional writing in the field of librarianship. While there is perhaps not as widespread agreement, it is also clear that there is a need to develop contributions to the professional literature from a wider range of librarians.

The conditions that presently exist do not contribute to the development of writing skills among librarians. The basic program of graduate library education is perhaps the only point at which any emphasis is placed on the development of writing skills. That emphasis is obviously somewhat limited, comes too early in an individual's professional career, and is not in a context in which writing is of primary concern. The present editorial practices of journal editors and publishers do not tend to contribute to an improvement of the situation. In virtually all cases proposed contributions are accepted or rejected on the basis of the existing content and presentation. Little or no advice is given to the authors on items that are rejected as to how the quality of their work could be improved. My personal experience, both as an author and an editor, indicates that there is very little opportunity for extensive editorial revision of works that are accepted for publication. In other words in most cases a librarian must present to an editor or publisher a finished product, produced on the basis of the individual's own writing skills and abilities, and have it accepted or rejected on that basis. The individual's work environment and professional associations do not generally allow for the development and improvement of writing skills. Existing work situations place most librarians in a directed setting where the emphasis is inevitably on the content of the work and not the presentation of ideas. In any case most librarians find themselves in work situations which allow for only limited contact with other professional librarians many of whom have either no interest in or no particular ability for writing. Professional associations and activities are, for the most part, too large and impersonal to allow for adequate direct personal interrelationships to develop which might have a real impact on the individual's professional growth and development in this as in other areas.

The result is that much of the professional growth and development of professional librarians that involves writing skills takes place in an individual framework with relatively little opportunity for the individual to discuss, review, and test his/her ideas and the way in which they are presented before putting them into final form for possible publication.

Within New England at the present time there appears to be a strong interest in the question of the improvement of professional writing on the part of academic librarians. This is evidenced by the excellent attendance at the Conference on Writing and Publishing for Librarians sponsored by the New England Chapter of the Association of College and Research Libraries that was held on April 4, 1975.

The formation and rapid growth of the New England Chapter of the Association of College and Research Libraries is evidence of the active interest on the part of academic librarians in this region in their professional growth and development. Attendance at and participation in meetings organized by ACRL-NEC has been excellent. The Executive Board of that organization has endorsed this proposal (see attached letter of endorsement). In addition, other activities and programs such as the New England Library Information Network (NELINET), the New England Library Board (NELB), and the annual meetings of the New England Library Association (NELA), and the New England College Librarians, have helped to create a strong climate of regional library activity. New England is a compact geographic area and it is very possible, therefore, for close and direct professional interactivity to occur within this region.

It is proposed therefore to establish, for a two-year period, a New England Academic Librarians' Writing Seminar that would identify a group of 10-12 professional librarians who could work together in a setting focussed specifically on the development and improvement of writing skills through group interaction under the direction of a professional librarian with demonstrated writing skills and abilities. This Seminar would seek to provide an alternative means for the continuing education of the participants in a structured, yet relatively informal setting, that would provide for the professional growth and development of the participants in the specific area of writing.

The Seminar would function on the basis of an initial two-day introductory working session, regular monthly one-day sessions, and four three-day intensive working sessions over the two-year period. Some of the details of procedures to be followed in the introductory working session and subsequent meetings are described briefly below. Part of the work of the Director of the Seminar would involve more detailed planning for the conduct and operation of the meetings of the participants. In addition to the meetings, arrangements would be developed for the interchange and review of written working documents by mail on a regular basis in the intervals between meetings.

The primary function of the Seminar would be to provide a setting in which the written work of the individuals could be reviewed and criticized on a continuing basis by the other participants. Through such interaction and critical review the writing skills and abilities of the individuals could be developed and improved and the immediate end products could be significantly improved in quality. The Seminar could help produce a better qualified body of contributors to the professional literature of librarianship over the next 25-30 years.

The director of the project would be Dr. Norman D. Stevens, University Librarian, of the University of Connecticut. Dr. Stevens has both an M. L. S. and a Ph. D. degree in Library Service from Rutgers University and has had experience as a library administrator at Howard University, Rutgers University, and the University of Connecticut. More importantly, Dr. Stevens has a demonstrated record as an author and editor which has provided him with the critical skills and abilities that are essential for the effective operation of the Seminar.

In order to provide the necessary focus and structure for the work two specific projects would be undertaken by the Seminar based on commitments from Mr. Eric Moon, President of the Scarecrow Press, and from Dr. Richard Dougherty, Editor of The Journal of Academic Librarianship. Specifically, it is proposed that members of the Seminar would produce a series of 10-12 short essays relating to the general topic of Unconsidered Aspects of Library Cooperation (e. g., cooperative sharing of personnel) to be published as a separate volume by the Scarecrow Press. It is also proposed that the members of the Seminar would produce a series of 10-12 short essays relating to the general topic of "A New Look at Old Problems" (e. g., the effective use of microforms) which would be published as a series in The Journal of Academic Librarianship. Both commitments are, of course, based on the assumption that the final quality of work produced will warrant publication. In order also to provide for more individual growth and development each participant would be expected to be engaged in at least one other substantial writing activity of his or her own choosing.

Because of the innovative nature of this program all of the procedural details cannot be described at this time. Many of those details would arise from the project and would be developed by the participants. The following, therefore, should be viewed as only a tentative statement of procedure. A detailed record of procedure would be maintained. The periodic and final reports to the Council would include a description of those working procedures.

If funding is available during the summer of 1976 the following timetable and procedures would be used to inform people of the program, to select applicants, and to organize and begin the work of the Seminar.

During the summer a brief description of the program and an application form would be prepared. That material would be distributed to academic librarians in New England using the ACRL-NEC mailing list. Copies would also be distributed directly to all academic libraries and graduate library schools in the region. In addition a short statement about the program would be developed as a news release. That news release would be sent both to the library press, with special emphasis on New England journals, as well as to the general newspapers in New England.

At the fall meeting of ACRL-NEC, which will be held in

conjunction with the annual meeting of the New England Library Association in September, an oral presentation of the program would be made and further material and applications distributed. Other direct presentations would be made as feasible and direct contact would be made with individual library directors and potential applicants in order to ensure adequate knowledge of the program.

Applications would be due by November 1, 1976. As part of the application each potential participant would be asked to submit a brief professional résumé, with special note of publications to date; one written piece of at least 3-4 pages on some aspect of librarianship which could be something already published, an internal library report, or a paper written for a library school course; and a statement endorsing participation in the program from his/her immediate supervisor. In addition each potential participant would be asked to include a brief (100-200 word) statement about why he/she wished to participate in the Seminar as well as a somewhat longer statement (up to 1000 words) about the writing activities that he/she would undertake as part of the program. This would include a statement on the main theme and the journal essay as well as on other activities that the potential participant might undertake.

Participants would not be expected to undertake research activities as a part of this program. It would be indicated, however, that they would be expected to have research already accomplished or underway which they might use in the context of this program.

The selection of the first participant, who would serve as Co-director, would be on the basis of demonstrated writing skills, as shown by a record of publication and an evaluation of the quality of that publication. That person would then be asked to review the applications of the remaining candidates with Dr. Stevens and they would jointly select the third participant. Demonstrated writing skills would not be required of the remaining participants. As additional participants were selected, they would be asked to assist in the review and selection process to the degree that it seemed advisable, and to the degree that time allowed, in order to insure selection of a harmonious working group.

Final selection of the participants would be accomplished by the end of December 1976 and the initial meeting would be held in January, 1977. The program would be expected to run through December, 1978.

The initial meeting would attempt to accomplish several things and would be designed to acquaint the participants with one another and to develop the basis for a close working relationship within the group. Special emphasis would be placed, therefore, on identifying means by which the potential problems of personal interrelationships presented by the fact that the focus of the Seminar would be on the critical analysis of each other's work could be overcome. While the Seminar would be primarily a self-directed program, it would be placed in the larger context of professional activities as appropriate.

Before the first meeting some articles on writing techniques and
practices, especially ones with a direct relationship to librarianship,
would be identified and distributed and those articles would be discussed at the first meeting. It is also possible that at the first
meeting, but it would more likely be at one of the subsequent intensive working sessions, at least one outside professional library jour-
nalist (i. e. , the editor of a major national professional journal) would
be asked to meet with the group to discuss writing techniques and
practices, and publication patterns and practices in librarianship,
and to review some of the work of the group. Finally some work
toward organizing the major work of the Seminar, the review and
criticism of ideas and written material, would be undertaken at the
initial meeting. As one example of an exercise that might be used
at that meeting the Director and Co-director could each write and
distribute first drafts of a short piece to participants. Prior to the
meeting they could then revise those pieces in their normal fashion
keeping all corrections and drafts. At the initial meeting the group
could then examine, criticize and rewrite those initial drafts. Comparison could then be made of the end product resulting from that
process and the end product resulting from the individual's normal
working process. The details of changes arrived at by both methods
could be reviewed and discussed.

Throughout the Seminar an emphasis would be placed on writing as a planned and organized activity with specific assignments and
deadlines to be met. At the initial meeting a tentative schedule for
the program would be developed. That schedule would be reviewed
and updated at each subsequent meeting. Regular meeting times and
places would be established, probably with a rotation of place in order
to avoid the dominance of the group by any one individual--including
the Director or Co-director--that might occur if the meetings were
regularly held at one institution.

In addition a schedule of expectations for each participant
would be developed by that participant in conjunction with the group.
This schedule would include a specific statement of what he/she accomplished within a given period of time. It also would be reviewed
and revised, if necessary, at each subsequent meeting. Each individual would be expected to serve on a rotating basis, as a liaison
for another individual in the group by establishing a pairing so that
they could make contact with each other at least weekly between
meetings to discuss and review their progress with meeting that
schedule.

Arrangements would be made for the exchange of drafts by
all participants between meetings and each participant would be expected to read and comment upon, in writing, on those drafts. At
each meeting a general review of progress would be held. In addition specific pieces would be identified as the topic for detailed analysis at each meeting. The person responsible for the work would
be expected to make a detailed presentation of his/her ideas and approaches and of the problems that have been encountered. Other
participants would have been expected to carefully review the material
beforehand and to have specific suggestions and comments to make.

Beyond the individual items produced as a result of the work of the Seminar, the members of the Seminar would seek to prepare at the end of the project a final report for the Council on Library Resources which would describe the project in detail, present a rec- ord of the work of the Seminar and its participants during the period of the project, and which would attempt to evaluate the impact of the Seminar on the professional growth and development of the individual participants. Finally it is expected that the Seminar, if it is success- ful, would continue, on the initiative of the participants, beyond the initial two-year period and that it would perhaps, especially as the initial participants leave, take on new members, and also that as individual participants relocate in other parts of the country, that it might serve as the basis for the development of similar undertak- ings in other locations.

June 21, 1976

DETAILED BUDGET

A. Salaries, Wages, and Employee Benefits
Secretary 50% $3,500 per annum January 1, 1977-December 31, 1978

Total	$7,000	Breakdown of benefits on $3,500. (20%)
Benefits	20%	
	$1,400	Life Insurance 1.5% $ 10.50
Total	$8,400	Unemployment &
		Workman's Com-
		pensation 3% 21.00
		FICA 22% 154.00
		Retirement 59% 413.00
		Hospitalization Ins.
		14.5% 101.50 $700.00

B. Consultant Fees
$200 a day for 2 days for participation in one meeting of the Seminar by a professional library journalist or editor.

C. Travel
This budget statement assumes 10 participants over a two-year period located within an average of 100 miles of the meeting location.

(1) Travel for attendance at meetings $6,000.
10 people x 200 miles x $.12 per mile = $240 per meeting
                                          25 meetings
                                         $6,000

(2) Lodging and meals
     luncheon at 20 one day meetings
        for 10 people = 200 luncheons
                            $4
                         $800 $800

     1 2-day session
        $14 per person - lodging
        $30 per person - meals
        $ 3 per person - registration
        $47 per person x 10 people = $470 $470

     4 3-day sessions
        $28 per person - lodging
        $45 per person - meals
        $ 3 per person - registration
        $76 per person x 10 people =
                    $760 per meeting
                       4 meetings
                 $3,040 $3,040

Reimbursement to the Program Director will be made in accordance
with standard state procedures for travel reimbursement.   Reimbursement to other participants will be made as an honorarium in
lieu of travel expenses at an average of $28 for one day sessions,
$47 for the 2-day session, and $76 for the 3-day session.

D. Supplies and Materials
    There will be some expenses, not borne by the University of
    Connecticut or the New England Chapter of the Association of
    College and Research Libraries, involved primarily in the prep-
    aration and distribution of notices about and applications for
    participation in the Seminar.   These are estimated at $1,500.

FIRST INTERIM REPORT
TO
COUNCIL ON LIBRARY RESOURCES

Introduction

This is the first interim report to the Council on Library Resources in connection with their grant to the University of Connecticut to support the New England Academic Librarians' Writing Seminar. It covers the period from the award of the grant on August 4, 1976 through the early part of January 1977. At this time the actual work of the Seminar is just scheduled to begin. This report, therefore, will deal exclusively with the steps that were taken to publicize the Seminar, to respond to inquiries, to consider and review applications, to select the participants, and to organize for the start of the Seminar.

Publicity

Upon notification of receipt of the grant, immediate steps were taken to publicize the grant in order to attract as large a number of qualified applicants as possible. Both a news release and a flyer describing the program were prepared for approval by the Council on Library Resources. After approval the news release was distributed through the University of Connecticut's Office of Public Information to newspapers in the region. It was also distributed directly by the Director of the Seminar to various national and regional library periodicals. These included: American Libraries, College and Research Library News, The Journal of Academic Librarianship, Library Journal, Wilson Library Bulletin, CALL, Channel, Bay State Librarian, Connecticut Libraries, Downeast Libraries, The Innocent Bystander (newsletter of the University of Connecticut Library), and the NELA Newsletter. In addition information about the program was sent to the three graduate library schools in New England at Simmons College, Southern Connecticut State College, and the University of Rhode Island as well as to all of the library associations in the six New England states. The response was good and information about the program appeared in at least seven places.

Three different mailing lists were obtained. A mailing list covering all libraries in New England was provided by the New England Research Application Center (NERAC) at the University of Connecticut. Two mailing lists were provided by the Association of College and Research Libraries, New England Chapter. The first was a mailing list of all of their members and the second was a list, which had been compiled through a survey, of all academic

librarians in New England employed in libraries which had participated in the survey. The lists were cross-checked to eliminate duplication and a total of 1, 917 flyers describing the program were
distributed directly to the academic libraries and librarians of New
England in September, 1976. Those 1, 917 flyers were sent according to the following geographic breakdown: Maine, 125; New Hampshire, 140; Vermont, 83; Massachusetts, 1, 055; Rhode Island, 137;
and Connecticut, 377.

As a result of the news items that appeared, a total of 44 inquiries, 23 of which were from outside New England, were received.
Copies of the flyer were distributed, with comments where appropriate, to all of those who so inquired.

On September 27, 1976 I addressed a business meeting of the
Association of College and Research Libraries, New England Chapter
that was held in Portsmouth, New Hampshire in connection with the
New England Library Association's annual meeting. A brief presentation of the Seminar was given to about 100 people, a number of questions were answered, and about a dozen copies of the flyer were distributed to people who had not already received one.

Applications

The actual number of final applications was somewhat less
than I had expected. A total of only 24 completed applications, including three from outside New England, were received. Those applications were summarized to provide information with which to review the applications for selection purposes. Based on conversations
held with a number of potential applicants, it would appear that the
requirements of the program in terms of the time demands were high
enough to discourage many people. Perhaps a larger number of applications would have been received if the program were of a shorter
duration and involved less writing, or if it were to provide for financial support that would allow for released time of some magnitude
for those participating in the Seminar.

Selection

Since there was no strong candidate with good previous writing
background, my initial plan to select one person as a Co-director
and then to work with that person in selecting additional participants
was dropped. Instead after a careful review of the applications I
concluded that there were three candidates who were obvious choices
for participation. They were notified of their selection and asked to
meet with me to review the remaining applications. With their assistance, an additional seven candidates were selected for the Seminar. There will be a total of twelve members of the Seminar, including myself.

Organization

During this initial period some steps were taken to organize
the work of the Seminar. Paperwork for the selection and hiring of
the half-time secretary was concluded; interviewing is now taking
place and it is expected that that person will begin work sometime
just before the end of January 1977. The Scarecrow Press and The
Journal of Academic Librarianship were notified of the receipt of the
grant and of my expectation that the Seminar will produce material
for them. They are being kept informed of progress as the Seminar
moves along and will, for example, receive copies of this and other
reports as well as more informal progress reports.

Arrangements have been made to hold the initial meeting of
the Seminar on January 20-21, 1977. Participants have been informed
of material that they are expected to prepare for that meeting and
an agenda for the meeting has been distributed to them. While information has been collected that will help determine the future meeting schedule, final work on establishing that schedule will be done at
the initial meeting.

The application of each member has been carefully reviewed
and I have written to each of them indicating what topics I would like
them to write on for the two directed projects. I have indicated that
I expect each of them to bring a draft statement describing in more
detail those topics to the initial meeting. The other major writing
project that each member will be engaged in has not yet been discussed and reviewed but will be covered at the initial meeting.

A bibliography of items pertaining to writing for library publications and the state of library literature has been compiled and
distributed. Each member has been asked to read that material and
it will form the basis for a brief discussion at the initial meeting.
At that time the Seminar will decide whether or not additional readings are needed and whether or not one or more textbooks or standard manuals on writing should be used in some way.

Full information about the Seminar has been distributed to
Arthur Plotnik, editor of American Libraries, and he has been asked
if he would be willing to participate in one of the longer meetings of
the Seminar. No response has yet been received. Richard Johnson,
editor of College & Research Libraries, has written to indicate his
interest in the Seminar and his willingness to be of assistance. Robert Stueart, Dean of the Library School at Simmons College, who has
written and spoken on the subject of professional writing, has also
indicated an interest in the Seminar and a willingness to participate.
Again at the first meeting the Seminar will decide what degree of
outside participation seems useful and how that might best be accomplished.

Next Steps

    The New England Academic Librarians' Writing Seminar is
ready to begin work and will do so at the end of this month.   The
emphasis of the Seminar will be on the prompt traslation of ideas
and research into written form for publication.   I fully expect to
have the general framework for the series of articles for The Journal of Academic Librarianship completed by the end of February 1977
and to have the introduction to and the first finished products for
that series completed by May 1977.

    I remain confident that the Seminar will be productive and that
it will produce relatively immediate results in terms of published
items.   Despite the limited number of applications I am pleased with
the quality of the members.   Some have published material before
but most have not to any great degree.   I look for the Seminar to
produce a substantial number of items of good quality over the next
two years and for it to permanently improve the writing skills and
the productivity of its members.

                                        January 9, 1977

SECOND INTERIM REPORT
TO
COUNCIL ON LIBRARY RESOURCES

Introduction

This is the second interim report to the Council on Library
Resources in connection with their grant to the University of Connecticut to support the New England Academic Librarians' Writing Seminar. It covers the period from January through July 1977. During
this time the initial meetings of the Seminar were held. This report
will deal with final participants, the meetings, progress, some organizational and procedural matters, and a tentative initial evaluation.

Final Participants

The members selected through the process identified in the
first interim report have all been participating fully in the work of
the Seminar with one exception. Although an effort was made to
include Alan E. Schorr, of the University of Alaska, as a special
participant in the program it was finally agreed, by mutual consent,
that that would not be feasible. He was dropped as a participant,
therefore, just as the Seminar was beginning. The subsequent work
of the Seminar seems to indicate that participation without regular
attendance at the meetings would not have been feasible in any case.

Meetings

Six meetings of the Seminar have been held to date. One was
a two-day organizational meeting at the W. Alton Jones campus of
the University of Rhode Island on January 20-21, 1977. Four one-
day meetings were held in February, March, April, and May, all
at the University of Connecticut in Storrs, Connecticut with the exception of the May meeting which was held at Durham, N. H. A
two-day meeting was held on June 29-30 at the Barney House of the
University of Connecticut in Farmington, Connecticut. That meeting
featured the attendance and participation of Mr. John Berry, editor
of the Library Journal.

Attendance at the meetings has been excellent; there have been
a total of only three absences all due to unavoidable circumstances.

Progress

The agendas and minutes of the meetings outline in some detail the work of the Seminar and are the main record of progress to
date.   One article has been published and is described in the attached
List of Publications which will serve on a continuing basis as the
main record of progress.   Ten other pieces, including the introduction and four essays for the proposed column in The Journal of Academic Librarianship, have been submitted for publication.   Two have
been accepted but have not yet been published.   The remaining eight,
which include The Journal of Academic Librarianship pieces, have
not yet been accepted.   Three more pieces for that series are in the
process of final revision and the remainder should be completed by
the fall of this year.

Other work is in progress as well and is reflected in the minutes.   There has been extensive discussion of the proposed book and
its contents.   Discussion has centered around the fact that in several
cases the topics initially suggested were artificial expressions of interest developed in relationship to the proposed overall topic.   It has
been decided to alter the approach to allow for individuals to write
on topics that relate more directly to their interests and to areas in
which they may be conducting research.

Organizational and Procedural Matters

The organization of the Seminar has taken some time at each
meeting and a considerable amount of time between meetings.   Basically there have been no problems or conflicts in this area.   The
procedures to be followed, on the other hand, have been the subjects
of considerable discussion in the Seminar and have undergone some
change.   That discussion and change have not appeared to unduly
hinder progress in the Seminar and generally has been one of mutual
agreement.

Tentative Evaluation

To this point I have been generally pleased with the work of
the Seminar and indications from the other participants are that they
have found the program useful.   However, no formal evaluation has
yet been undertaken.   In the initial six months the members of the
group have established a good personal working relationship with one
another and there appears to be an increasingly active interchange of
ideas.   There seems to be a ready acceptance of the criticism that
is offered.   Certainly the written work that has been produced has
shown substantial improvement from first draft to final product.   It
has been somewhat more difficult than I had expected to stimulate the
interests of the participants in producing written material, especially
of a more extensive nature.   The pieces for The Journal of Academic
Librarianship have come about on the schedule I had anticipated.
There have been fewer additional pieces written than I had expected

and to some degree they have been shorter and more general than I might have liked.   The production of the longer essays for the book has not yet begun and will require a major effort starting in September of 1977 if they are all to be completed by the end of 1978.

July 29, 1977

THIRD INTERIM REPORT
TO
COUNCIL ON LIBRARY RESOURCES

Introduction

This is the third interim report to the Council on Library Resources in connection with their grant to the University of Connecticut to support the New England Academic Librarians' Writing Seminar. It covers the period from August 1977 through January 1978.

Meetings

During this period six one-day meetings of the Seminar were
held in September, October, November, and December 1977 and January 1978 at various locations in New England. No meetings were
held in July or August 1977 because of the complications of summer
vacation schedules. Attendance at the meetings has been good although there have been more absences than in the initial six months
of the Seminar.

Progress

The agendas and minutes of the meetings outline in some detail the work of the Seminar during this period. Six pieces are being
considered for publication and a few others have been accepted and
are awaiting publication. Given the generally long delays in publication it is creditable that six articles have actually been published in
the first year of the Seminar's existence.

The essays for The Journal of Academic Librarianship have
now substantially been completed and have been submitted. They
should appear on schedule during the early part of 1978.

Primary emphasis is now being placed on the preparation of
the essays for the book. Several of those have been begun and a
detailed schedule of completion is now being developed. It is difficult to judge progress at this point but it appears as though the work
will proceed on schedule.

Organizational and Procedural Matters

During the period covered by this report there have been no
major changes in organization or procedure as things seem to be

working reasonably well in that regard.   Some minor changes and
adaptations have been made.

Tentative Evaluation

    I remain generally pleased with the work of the Seminar and
the other participants continue to express their satisfaction.   We are
beginning to discuss matters relating to a more formal evaluation of
the Seminar and will, towards the end of the Seminar, attempt such
an evaluation.   The cohesiveness of the Seminar has continued to develop and there has been a noticeable change in the level of and acceptance of criticism which is valuable.

Other Comments

    During the period covered by this report there have been sev-
eral developments either directly or indirectly related to the work
of the Seminar that warrant mention.

    (1) Ms. Susan Lindgren, one of the participants, and a librar-
ian from the Shippensburg State College Library, where Mr. Scott
Bruntjen, another participant, works, exchanged jobs for a period of
two weeks.

    (2) I have been asked to serve as moderator for a panel dis-
cussion on professional publishing to be sponsored by the Nassau
County Library Association in March of 1978.

    (3) As a result of an approach made to me several members
of the Seminar are now tentatively scheduled to participate in a program on writing and publishing by librarians to be sponsored by the
College and University Library Section of the Connecticut Library
Association at the annual CLA meeting in April of 1978.

                            February 7, 1978

FOURTH INTERIM REPORT
TO
COUNCIL ON LIBRARY RESOURCES

Introduction

This is the fourth interim report to the Council on Library
Resources in connection with their grant to the University of Connecticut to support the New England Academic Librarians' Writing Seminar. It covers the period from February 1978 through July 1978.
A brief interim report will subsequently be provided to cover the
final period from August 1978 through December 1978 in addition to
the final report for the project.

Meetings

During this period five one-day meetings and one two-day
meeting of the Seminar were held in various locations in New England. The two-day meeting was held in April in conjunction with the
annual meeting of the Connecticut Library Association. That allowed
S. Bruntjen, B. Hill, and N. Stevens to participate in a program on
writing and publishing by librarians sponsored by the College and
University Library Section of the Connecticut Library Association.
The other members of the Seminar attended that program meeting
as well. The program was attended by about 75 persons and was
well received. A special meeting with Mr. Richard Dougherty, editor of The Journal of Academic Librarianship, to discuss that journal
and its editorial practices was held in May.

Progress

The agendas and minutes of the meetings outline in some detail the work of the Seminar during this period. The essays for
The Journal of Academic Librarianship continue to appear and have
elicited noticeable response from readers that has resulted in the
publication of several letters to the editor and one counter-essay,
and the tentative scheduling of a second counter-essay.

Several other pieces, primarily by the Director, have been
published but work by other members is either under review or in
progress of publication. A bibliography of publications is attached.

Primary emphasis continues to be placed on the preparation
of the book. A draft of all of the introductory and auxiliary materials has been completed and reviewed. Two essays are in the final

editing process and one other is nearly to that stage.   It appears as though all pieces will be completed by late 1978 or early 1979.   A tentative target date which would call for delivery of the completed manuscripts to The Scarecrow Press by March 1, 1979 has been set.

Organizational and Procedural Matters

No substantial changes have been made in the way in which the Seminar operates as things continue to work reasonably well.   It is not anticipated that any changes will be made in the final stages of the Seminar.

August 1, 1978

FIFTH INTERIM REPORT
TO
COUNCIL ON LIBRARY RESOURCES

Introduction

This is the fifth interim report to the Council on Library Resources in connection with their grant to the University of Connecticut in support of the New England Academic Librarians' Writing Seminar. It covers the period from August 1978 through January 1979.
This is the last interim report and will be followed by a final report
at the conclusion of the project on June 30, 1979.

During the period covered by this report the work of the Seminar was relatively light for two reasons. First the Director of the
Seminar was heavily engaged in work relating to the move of the University of Connecticut Library to a new building and was unable to
devote much time directly to the Seminar. In addition the individual
members of the Seminar were engaged in writing the longer pieces
that will make up the book to be published as the final work of the
Seminar. Thus their work largely consisted in writing rather than
in review and discussion.

Meetings

Only two meetings of the Seminar were held; one was held in
September and the other in October. At those meetings the drafts
of several of the book essays were reviewed in detail. Discussion
of several other brief pieces was also held.

Progress

The agendas and the minutes of those two meetings do not
fully represent the work of the Seminar during this period. As was
indicated, most of the time was devoted to individual writing of the
longer pieces. All of the essays in The Journal of Academic Librarianship series "On Our Minds" have now appeared. Several other
pieces were also published and a complete listing of the publications
emanating from the Seminar to date is attached.

For reasons mentioned above the completion of the book has
been delayed. The introductory material has been completed and two
essays have been completed. Most of the remaining eight are in
draft form and have been at least partially reviewed. It is now anticipated that all of the essays will be completed by the official date

of the end of the project and that the manuscript will be submitted to Scarecrow Press no later than August 1, 1979.

At the start of September 1978 one of the participants, Susan Lindgren, left her position at the University of Vermont Library to enter a Master's in Business Administration program at the University of Arizona. Ms. Lindgren had hoped to continue in the project through the exchange of mail and tapes but her workloads and the distance involved have not made that possible. She has now, in effect, dropped out of the Seminar in the sense that she will not be completing an essay for the book.

Organizational and Procedural Matters

No changes have been made in the way in which the Seminar operates. A two-day meeting is scheduled for early February for review of progress to date. It is anticipated that much of the work of review and editing of the book essays after that meeting will be carried out by mail.

Next Steps

In the initial proposal for the Seminar it had been suggested that the work of the Seminar might continue on an informal basis after the formal completion of its work. While that has not been discussed in detail in the Seminar it now appears unlikely that that will, in fact, take place. At most an informal exchange of ideas, and perhaps written materials, may take place among a few members of the Seminar.

Tentative Evaluation

All of the essays for The Journal of Academic Librarianship have been completed and published. The ability to have all 11 members of the Seminar complete those essays and have them published was a considerable accomplishment. All of those essays required considerable revision and editing which the Seminar participants accomplished; there is no question but what the final products represented a substantial improvement over the first drafts. The participants produced fewer additional written published pieces than had been anticipated but a number of such items were completed and published. The work involved in that process was an excellent learning experience for the participants. A more complete evaluation will be provided in the final report.

February 3, 1979

FINAL REPORT
TO
COUNCIL ON LIBRARY RESOURCES

Introduction

This is the final report to the Council of Library Resources
in connection with their grant to the University of Connecticut in support of the New England Academic Librarians' Writing Seminar. It
provides information on the work of the Seminar from the date of
the Fifth Interim Report (February 1979) through the formal conclusion of the grant (June 30, 1979) and beyond. In addition it provides
a final summary of the work of the Seminar.

Work Since Fifth Interim Report

Since the Fifth Interim Report the work of the Seminar has
continued to concentrate on the conclusion of the essays that will
constitute the book to be published by Scarecrow Press. Not much
other work has been carried out within the context of the Seminar.

Two meetings were held. The first, a two-day meeting, was
held in February 1979 and the second, a one-day meeting, was held
in August 1979. In general those meetings have concentrated on the
review of the book essays. In the intervals between meetings the
Director has concentrated on following up with letters and phone calls
in an effort to see that the final essays are completed.

The initial deadlines mentioned in the Fifth Interim Report
have proven to be elusive but it now appears as though the work is
indeed reaching a conclusion and that the completed manuscript will,
in fact, be submitted to Scarecrow Press sometime this fall.

No further changes were made in the way in which the Seminar
operated during the period covered by this report. It is expected
that in concluding the work of the Seminar that the final versions of
the book essays will be distributed by mail and that comments will
be exchanged by mail. No further meetings are scheduled.

Final Report

In one sense even this is not a complete final report. As a
part of the book to be published a more complete report on the history, work, and evaluation of the Seminar will be prepared. That
should be construed as the complete final report of the Seminar.

Copies of that book will be forwarded to the Council in fulfillment of
the requirements for a final report.   This semi-final report is largely intended to provide coverage of the work during the last period of
the project, to provide a cover document for the final financial reporting by the University of Connecticut, and to provide a general
summary of the work of the Seminar.   It does include, as an attach-
ment, a complete listing of the publications emanating from the Seminar to date but again that will be updated by a more complete listing
in the final book publication.

The Interim reports submitted to date and the report that will
be prepared for the book largely cover the background and description
of the Seminar from its inception to its completion.

In general the Seminar seems to have achieved its primary
objectives and to have provided some training and experience in
writing for publication for the participants.   As is perhaps true with
many projects, it did not completely fulfill expectations.   Somewhat
fewer pieces, in addition to those specifically planned for, were published by members of the Seminar (other than the Director) than had
been anticipated.   It took longer to complete the work of the Seminar
than had been projected.   Based on a tentative evaluation, it appears
that most members of the Seminar are not likely to continue to write
material for publication on a regular basis.   On the other hand it
does appear that at least two members of the Seminar will continue
to be active in this respect to a degree greater than they had previously.   It also seems clear that for almost all of the members of
the Seminar participation in the program has strengthened their writing skills and has given them greater confidence in their writing
abilities.   This clearly will be useful to them to the extent to which
their jobs require the use of those skills.   It also seems likely that
they will all feel more inclined to venture to write for publication
should an idea or issue arise in which they have a particular interest.
Finally it appears unlikely that much continuing contact will occur
between members of the Seminar on a regular basis as had been anticipated; nor does it seem likely that the experience of the individual
participants will encourage them to share the interests and skills
that they have acquired with others.   Some continuing contact will
occur on a limited basis and it is hoped that the interests and skills
gained may be shared with others as particular needs occur.

Conclusion

The support of the Council on Library Resources for the New
England Academic Librarians' Writing Seminar was both welcome and
helpful.   The Council's willingness to support a program designed to
encourage the development of skills by librarians that will assist
them in their career development seems to me to be of considerable
value and to provide a return which, while it is difficult to measure,
potentially can far exceed the investment.   From my perspective as
a library administrator, such continued support for similar programs
is something that I would hope the Council would be able to fund.

From the perspective both of a library administrator and as Director
of this particular project it appears as though one of the greatest
difficulties is how librarians can effectively participate in such programs given the constraints and limitations of their job assignments.
In the case of this Seminar, for example, it is likely that the work
would have been more productive had the program provided for some
degree of released time for the participants.   On a day-to-day basis,
however, such activities as writing for publication must normally be
accomplished within the context of a full work-week and full work-
year.   In that respect I have no immediate suggestions but I do feel
that it is a general issue that the Council might seek to address,
not just in terms of this kind of project but in terms of its support
for library staff development programs as well as in terms of general academic library support and encouragement of staff growth and
development.

August 27, 1979